Divorced Fathers

Divorced Fathers

Reconstructing a Quality Life

Thomas Oakland, Ph.D.

Department of Educational Psychology
The University of Texas at Austin

with contributions from

Nancy Voight Wedemeyer, Ph.D.
Austin, Texas

Edwin J. Terry, Jr., J.D.
Austin, Texas

Jane Manaster
Austin, Texas

 **HUMAN SCIENCES PRESS, INC.**
72 FIFTH AVENUE,
NEW YORK, N.Y. 10011

Printed in the United States of America
456789 98765432

Library of Congress Cataloging in Publication Data

Oakland, Thomas.
  Divorced fathers.

  Includes index.
  1. Divorced fathers—United States. 2. Father and child—United States. 3. Children of divorced parents—United States. 4. Custody of children—United States.
  I. Title.
HQ756.O24   1983   306.8'9   83-93
ISBN 0-89885-101-7

This book is dedicated to David and Chris for encouraging me to work toward realizing my most important goal—to be a good father.

Contents

Introduction   **9**

1. **Life after Divorce:**
   A Reconstruction Project   **11**
   Divorce in Context   14
   The Dimensions of Divorce   19
   A Special Dimension: Time   23

2. Your Psychological and Social Changes
   Passages through Divorce   27

3. Understanding Your Children   51
   Three Theories of Behavior   52
   Basic Needs   53

4. Divorce: Its General Effects on Children   65
   Children's Passages through **Divorce**   67
   Factors Influencing Children's Adjustment   74
   Preparing Children for the Divorce   81

5. Anticipating Children's Problems
   and Providing Help   85
   Signs of Stress in Children   88

6. Child Custody: A Central Issue   105
   What Has Been Traditionally Done   106
   Sole Custody   108
   Split Custody   115
   Joint Custody or Co-Parenting   118
   Difficult Issues   122
   Conclusion   128

7. Basic Legal Issues: Before You Begin   131
   Alternatives to Divorce   131
   Types of Divorces   133
   The Lawyer   135
   Problems and Prejudices
     in the Legal System   138

8. Untying the Legal Knots:
     Preparing for a Divorce   141
   Preparing Yourself for Legal Action   142
   Grounds for Divorce   143
   Determining Custody   143

9. Keeping the Knots Untied:
     Living within the Law   151
   Custody and Visitation   153
   Custody Can Be Changed   156

10. Managing Your Household   161
    Foods   162
    Life Beyond the Kitchen   174

11. Budgeting   185

Index   199

Introduction

Except for death, no other human experience is more feared or causes greater stress than divorce. Divorce brings a confluence of events— social, emotional, sexual, financial, vocational, and legal—all of which occur suddenly and have a tremendous impact. Life becomes more of a struggle, and each day seems filled with new challenges. While most challenges can be handled effectively, some are overwhelming.

This book is written for fathers experiencing divorce-related difficulties who want to fashion a better life for themselves and their children. In it, you will learn that a father's adjustment and that of his children are inseparably intertwined; that quality of their relationships is a most important factor in future happiness; and that fathers should try to continue wholesome relationships with their children, to make plans and sacrifices to achieve this, and to press assertively for their rights and those of their children.

Although progress through this period is not easy, it is facilitated when three conditions are present: fathers should be informed, should have a life plan for themselves and their children, and should be motivated and disciplined.

This book presents information on various problems and issues fathers and children experience as a result of divorce, and offers various suggestions which, when followed, are likely to help fathers and children develop healthy, happy, and productive lives.

The information should allow fathers to anticipate what lies ahead for them and their children and to plan effectively for their futures. Proper planning is needed to identify problems, resources, and solutions. A business, to be successful, must have some goals and directions. This also holds true for fathers and families.

Goals, once formed, become a plan for action. The action itself comes through motivation and self-discipline. Motivation provides the springboard, the will, and the energy to accomplish what needs to be done. This book tries to emphasize a "can-do" attitude used successfully by hundreds of thousands of fathers in going through this period.

Discipline is represented by the strength of convictions and commitment to live a life following certain rules and standards. Self-control must be maintained in spite of setbacks and defeats. Motivation becomes the energizer and discipline, the control. Both are needed to take charge of life and direct it toward healthy and happy pursuits.

As a divorced father, expect to find that you must work harder to earn the parenthood that fathers of intact families customarily take for granted. However, the rewards will be immeasurable. Hopefully, you will find this book helpful in this important pursuit.

1

Life After Divorce

A Reconstruction Project

Nancy Voigt Wedemeyer

Divorce is one of the most stressful events anyone can experience. It brings changes to virtually all personal aspects of your life. It changes the ways you relate to your children and requires you to find different ways of taking care of your physical, social, emotional, intellectual, and spiritual needs. It means reassessing the things that are going well and poorly in your life and reorganizing them so that more things go better. It means disrupting or losing much that is familiar and entering new territories that sometimes are exciting, overwhelming, and frustrating. All of these conditions must be faced and dealt with in the midst of large social pressures. In addition to these personal issues, you will also be affected by inflation and less income, legal changes in your family, and new social expectations of how single parents should behave.

Life after divorce resembles rebuilding a house damaged by a tornado. The velocity of some tornadoes is mild. While damage occurs, the basic structure remains intact. Rebuilding can begin immediately with few new materials needed. Life goes on somewhat normally.

However, the velocity of other tornadoes, like some divorces, is more wicked and rampant. Not much is left intact. Only the foundation and some walls or plumbing may be salvageable. There are memories of what the structure looked like and pictures to prove it. There is hope to rebuild life somewhat as it was but with improvements.

At first, the task seems overwhelming. There is more debris than order. After the storm has passed, you have to examine the remains to find out what can be used again and what has been too damaged. It isn't always clear where and how to find reconstruction materials. You are disappointed to discover that relatives and friends do not rush to your aid. Many seem preoccupied with their own needs and are not readily sympathetic. Various experts are ready to help, but some seem primarily motivated to make a profit from you rather than to consider your needs first. And, in the meantime, you face an avalanche of questions: Where do I live? What clothes do I have? Where do I eat? What are my chldren doing? When can I see them again? Why did this thing have to happen to me, anyway?

After the initial shock of divorce and a period of self-pity, many men realize that handling a major reconstruction project, be it a shattered building or a shattered life, is a a matter of organization and problem-solving skills. You have demonstrated these skills before, and you can do it again, even though the task is large.

There are seven basic steps to good problem solving:
- Identify the problem.
- Generate possible solutions.
- Evaluate alternatives.
- Choose the best one.
- Identify a strategy for obtaining that solution.
- Try it.
- Evaluate the results, and, if necessary, start all over.

Problem solving requires specific and focused action, but that action is always within a larger context. When there are multiple problems, as there are in divorces, problem solving still is viable, even though a bit harder. A *foreground-background* technique helps. Before beginning to deal with a situation needing improvement, examine the whole picture. Look over the full range of problems. Notice their interactions. Can some problems be resolved only by first attending to others? For instance, you may need regular eating and sleeping patterns before you can tackle other things.

Problems may exist in a number of areas: financial; vocational; relationships with your children and former wife, and other family members; food and housing; medical, psychological, emotional, and sexual. A problem in one area often corresponds with problems in others. Some problems are more solvable than others. These should be brought into the foreground first. Successful problem solving can occur when the resources that enable a problem to be resolved are present. Instead of being frozen into inaction, identify some basic problem which you can deal with and which interests you. For example, tackle some basic needs like food and housing. You have some control over these. Moreover, once these basics fall into place, you can go on to handle the more complex and difficult concerns.

Set up a general master plan which will guide your problemsolving. Choose one problem to bring into the foreground and to work on first. This problem should be basic but not too large nor too distasteful so that it will help smooth the way to your handling other problems. Focus on resolving this problem and push the others into the background. When you are satisfied with the solution, push it into the background, and survey the whole picture again. Then choose another problem to bring into the foreground to focus on.

Each time you are ready to change what is in focus and what is in the background, observe the progress you are making in straightening up the whole picture. Pat yourself on the back for the progress you have made, and be patient with your backsliding. Research indicates that it often takes four or five years to work through all the aspects of divorce.

As you rebuild your life after divorce, it helps to get good information about potential problems and possible solutions. That is what this book is about. This chapter will give an overview. Other chapters will focus in more detail on some of the problems which other divorced fathers have found particularly challenging.

DIVORCE IN CONTEXT

To look at the big picture, you need to understand its various parts. Divorce is a disruption of family life, and to understand it requires some understanding of contemporary family life in the U.S. Not only are there more divorces today, but the meaning of getting divorced and the ways of handling it are rapidly changing. There is a strong trend toward "no-fault" divorce in which the spouses agree to end the marriage without attempting to prove that one of them is solely responsible by having failed to live up to his or her marital obligations. This greater recognition of joint responsibility for the failure of a marriage also seems to be affecting the post-divorce circumstances. Many states are moving away from perpetual alimony and the idea that a man is always obligated to support the woman financially. Spouses often are expected to take care of themselves financially after the separation. Also, more fathers are maintaining closer contacts with their children after divorce and gaining joint or full custody of them. These trends can be healthy and are related to changes in the meaning and patterns of family life in the whole society. Understanding these changes gives insight into both the increased number of divorces and the new ways of rebuilding lives affected by divorce.

Contemporary Changes in U.S. Family Life

Scholars of the family describe its changes today in terms of reductions and transformations of the traditional expectations people had of the family. Over the centuries and in most societies, people have looked to the family to fulfill several basic functions: to protect, support, encourage, nurture, and love in a functional and continuous manner; also, to provide food, clothing, and shelter. The family constitutes an economic unit that defines the roles and status of its members, as well as being the center of regulation of sexual behavior and continued reproduction of the species, the key focus of child-rearing responsibilities, and the institution for developing social and emotional characteristics.

Modern technology has dramatically altered many of these functions by removing them from the family and reassigning them to new, specialized institutions or by enabling individuals to carry them out alone. The needs traditionally met by families still exist, but more and more they are being met differently and outside of the family. For example, children still must be born for the species to continue, but medical and public health advances have so radically decreased infant and child mortality rates and extended the life span that fewer offspring per individual will still insure the continuation of the species. Sex for procreation has, therefore, become less important. Economic productivity no longer requires physical strength but does require specialized intellectual and skills training. Thus, men are no longer biologically superior for all vocations. Furthermore, vocational training is so complex it can no longer be carried out in the generalized setting of the home.

These factors have combined to undermine the traditional roles of all adults. There is little need or support for women to be dedicated to full-time childbearing and child rearing. This occupies the time and energy of only some and even those who do raise children are so occupied only for some 18 to 25 years of their 50 years of adulthood. These changes have led many women to jobs outside of the home and to the demand for societal status based on their performance in these jobs rather than in their role as wives and mothers. Concomitantly, men are being pressured to participate more actively at home and with their children. These changes bring the traditional post-divorce child support and custody patterns into question.

Modern technology has also brought unprecedented affluence. The richness and variety of available choices have led to a demand for a materialistic life style that also has created pressures for changing traditional family life. Frequently, both parents work in order to attain the life style they wish, more families utilize convenience foods or eat out, standards of housekeeping are lowered, and children increasingly are sent to day-care and after-school baby sitters.

The parental role is being described more as that of an executive than a caregiver. Fathers and mothers are both being expected to take responsibility for all facets of home. Cooking, cleaning, and other household activities may be performed by either the husband or wife. Husbands and wives are developing social relationships with friends and colleagues of both sexes at work, and there often is little time or energy left in either spouse to arrange joint entertaining at home. Thus, there is a diffusion of activities which used to have a clear family focus.

Some theorists suggest that the only major function left for families today is to provide the emotional support found only in intimate personal relationships, but even this is questioned. Some researchers have documented the difficulty of emotional relationships being carried out in the narrow context of today's small mother-father-two-children families. The intensity of "togetherness," in fact, may undermine emotional growth and security. The shift toward emphasizing the individual in the pop culture of the 1960s and 1970's clearly is also evident. This has been described as the "me" generation. The idea of maturity as an ability to compromise and be a part of sustaining groups has given way to an ideal of maximizing individual potential.

Many of these changes are behind the rapid increase in the number of divorces. Couples who get married without giving serious thought to the relationship may get caught between their individual needs and the demands of a traditional family life and find themselves unable to maintain the marriage relationship. Others have been caught in significant societal shifts in which the rules they expected to govern their married life no longer apply. The husband or wife may not understand the new rules or feel comfortable with them. Frequently, the willingness to initiate changes in rules develops at different rates. Such confusions add to the difficulties in resolving a divorce.

The major changes in family life and the increasing rate of failure in marriage have brought renewed attention to the study of family life. Within the past decade new ways have been developed for understanding how families function. The family's dynamic factors and basic processes have been stressed rather than its conventional roles and forms.

New Understandings of Family Life

New approaches to studying the family emphasize what is "healthy" rather than what is "normal." Normal is neutral in terms of values. Normal means what is typical and most commonly done. Healthy has ethical implications. Healthy means what is good, what is nourishing for people. For marriages to fall apart has become almost normal. Given the pain and unhappiness associated with most divorces, for marriages to fall apart does not seem healthy.

Discovering what makes families healthy becomes part of a blueprint useful in rebuilding a healthy life after divorce. Healthy families in our society (and nourishing individual life styles) are basically characterized by two factors. The first factor is an emotional climate which provides a sense of closeness and support, yet leaves room for individuality. The second factor is the balance between enough predictability and structure to provide a sense of stability and enough openness and flexibility to adapt to new circumstances as they arise.

These factors are both interpersonal and dynamic; that is, they arise from daily interactions with people and events and continually change within those people and events. They are not states which can be built and then left alone. They always require attention. Divorce usually comes when there is a crisis in at least one of these factors, and it usually creates an even greater crisis.

A healthy emotional climate exists when each person in the family feels important to the group. This includes the person's ability to express his or her opinions and feelings and the ability of others within the group to accept what the others say with respect and care. Many divorces occur when one spouse feels that his or her feelings no longer are respected or cared about.

A divorce brings about a situation where someone is no longer *expected* to care. New relationships must be built. Building new relationships always takes time and tends to be frustrating and risky. Overtures toward new relationships are often rejected but the efforts must continue.

Starting to build emotional support over again is also different from starting from scratch. There is a legacy from a previous strong emotional relationship. Emptiness feels even more empty after you experience fullness. Old patterns of sharing with a specific person and counting on her to care are hard to break. Divorced spouses often cling to the few positive feelings that existed between themselves. Fantasies (the "what if's") replace reality (the "what are's"). Or, divorced spouses may be angry at each other for no longer providing the accustomed support. A man may view his former mate as being out to get him in any way she can. Disentangling yourself from these emotions often takes several years. But you aren't ready to enter fully into new relationships until you have resolved the old ones.

Other difficulties arise when you have children. It is very damaging when children are psychologically abandoned while their parents are separating. Yet breaking completely away from your ex-spouse emotionally is made more difficult when you try to maintain close relationships with your children because of the continued contact necessary.

Starting over after a divorce can mean that you do not return to scratch, but that you continue your life by maintaining the good aspects and discarding the bad. Transactional analysis talks about the tapes we retain over the years and play back to ourselves. You may choose to edit your past so as to emphasize your weaknesses, tragedies, and unhappiness. Or you can choose to edit your experiences to highlight your strengths and happiness. You probably are somewhat settled professionally and personally and do not have a need for total major changes. With age, you have acquired wisdom and maturity. People have loved and cared for you and will continue to do so. Profit from your past and emphasize those parts which promote strength and happiness.

Finding the right balance between stability and flexibility is also a complex and continuing process for healthy families. Circumstances change. Children grow up, you meet new people, you may change jobs, or incur a major illness. These and other factors will always be present to disrupt your stability. On the other hand, a life which is overly constant and stable can lead to rigidity and the inability to adjust to challenges. No one is the same person he was

10 years ago. Healthy families and people constantly are making small adjustments, for continually adjusting patterns of cooperation and responsibilities are more apt to weather storms successfully. Nervous breakdowns occur when people have not made the small but important day-to-day changes, and their system becomes unable to handle the cumulative changes.

Yet, a divorce creates great instability by ending many familiar routines of time, place, and personal relationships. Reconstructing your life after divorce often involves a major reconstruction of the basic components of stability.

One way to gain stability is to avoid preventable major changes. Some men unwisely leave their family and friends, change jobs, and move away after a divorce. This generally is not healthy because it leads to further instability. Examine those parts of your life which are both good and stable. Maintain these forms of support. Make changes only where they are necessary.

THE DIMENSIONS OF DIVORCE

The dimensions of divorce involve the many parts of your life which were intertwined with marriage and family. Because marriage and family life serve many functions, divorce involves many dimensions. Some are fairly pragmatic. Others are quite subtle and psychological. Some reflect emptiness and loss while others suggest new demands which must be mastered. In rebuilding your life after divorce, you eventually must deal with all of them.

Legal Factors

Divorce is a legal act. It changes one's marital status and brings attendant changes in rights and responsibilities. Many people tend to view the legal aspects of divorce as mechanical and fairly unimportant. Yes, the most basic changes are worked out in your day-to-day behavior. However, once divorced, the law is your constant companion. The divorce decree has the force of law, and its terms are binding and difficult to change. It is important to think through the implications of property, child custody, and child visitation agreements *before* accepting a final divorce decree. Obtain good legal counsel to help you know and protect your rights. See Chapters Note and Note for more complete discussion of legal issues.

Emotional Support

High-quality emotional relationships are a central notion to marriages and families. Most often, the expectation of emotional support is what makes marriage appealing. And it is the deterioration of the emotional relationship between spouses that typically leads to divorce. If you have experienced positive loving support at one time in your marriage, you are apt to feel its loss very strongly. In addition to the sense of loss, many divorced people feel great anger that they are personally experiencing the problems of divorce in the first place, and also some guilt at causing other people to suffer loss as well.

As a married person you were probably used to (or at least expected to find) mutual support from your spouse. You took care of her in some important ways, and she took care of you in other ways. As a divorced person, you find that no one has a total commitment to you, and you need to find support from different sources for different needs. What do you do when you need to talk with someone? Who do you know now who might be willing to listen or to share answers? Or where might you find someone? What kind of contact if any, do you want with your ex-wife, your relatives, your friends?

Domestic Tasks

Even if you helped a lot with household and child-care tasks when you were married, it is different to hold the full responsibility alone. Logistics is a major key. When these things are organized, they are not too difficult to carry out. But, without planning, such minor things as running out of soap or toilet paper, or not having clean clothes on hand, can become constant irritations. People under stress need to keep most routine and mundane issues in the background in order to concentate on more demanding tasks. Keep household tasks routine and in the background. Chapter Note and

Note provide some guidelines to help you keep domestic chores done and in the background.

Finances

Two probably can't really live as cheaply as one, even when you live in the same household, but you certainly can't while supporting two households. Few fathers realize the financial strain divorce brings until they experience it directly. Some states still require alimony. Child support is required in virtually all divorces in which there are dependent children. Writing off a check every month puts a noticeable dent in almost any income. With today's inflation rates, there are pressures to set the amounts high or to raise them later. In addition, you turn your money over to your former spouse—with whom you are angry and displeased—and have no chance to say how it is spent.

Another way in which divorce affects finances is by interfering with career aspirations. When lots of energy is going into personal problems, job performance suffers. Your employer may tolerate your low productivity and preoccupation only so long. By assuming major child-care responsibility, you also put your career at a disadvantage. You may even secretly wish to be fired to be out of a job with no money. Then, you think, the courts would not allow the S.O.B. to take your last dime. When you're down and out, someone will rescue you.

How will you pay for your obligations to your first family and still provide for yourself or a second family? Do you want or need to make changes in your life style or your career plans? Might a promotion involve a transfer away from your children? How do you feel about the disruption it will cause in your relationships? How much long-distance communication (phone calls, plane tickets) can you afford to support? Do you really want to climb the career ladder at the expense of other life benefits?

Relations With Your Children

Your relationships with your children are certain to change after the divorce. For many men there is a dramatic reduction in the amount of time they are allowed to see their children. In fact, their parental rights typically are terminated, and they are reduced to a visitor role. Most children from divorced families have more access to their neighbors than to their fathers. And the courts typically have created this situation. Until the laws and attitudes of judges change, there may be little you can do about visitation and other rights without the cooperation of your ex-wife. For fathers and children who have been close, divorce can be extremely cruel.

Times are changing for divorced fathers. The caricature of the woman getting the house, car, and children, and the man getting the bills fortunately is being erased, albeit slowly. Men are increasingly choosing to press assertively for their rights and those of their children. Efforts to bring about needed sexual equality in social and vocational areas also serve to remove women's most-favored status in divorces. Courts increasingly are granting men child custody, child support, and even alimony. More and more fathers are willingly expressing their desire for wholesome relationships with their children and are able to make some plans and sacrifices to achieve this.

You should realize, however, that fathers who obtain or share custody will still experience major changes in their relationships with their children. The children will have to adjust to the custody and visitation agreements, and this will affect you. Children may pout, fuss, be angry at you, or ignore you. They will be interested in and probably a bit resentful of new friends or activities you become involved with. And while they are with you, there will be a shift from joint to sole responsibility in the many practical demands of child care, such as food, clothing, shelter, and friends. These requirements and each child's wishes for a relationship with you do not remain static but change over time.

Fathers entering the period of separation are likely to face hundreds of questions. What kind of time can I reasonably (and legally) spend with my children? What activities do we want to do? Can I develop a normal, full parent-child relationship if I get to see them only infrequently? If I can't have a close personal relationship with them, is it right to expect me to be the financial provider? To what degree do I want to continue to share information and insights concerning the children with their mother? How do I want to handle our children's feelings for her and me? How do I want to relate to the children's relatives both on my side and their mother's side?

Each is important. All questions may never be fully resolved. Each involves at least one other party—frequently an ex-spouse or a child. Even if you act responsibly, others may be unable or unwilling to cooperate in seeking good solutions.

Socializing

This is another area in which significant changes will occur. You are now an "eligible man" and will be welcomed in many social situations. This can be flattering and open up many rewarding opportunities, but recognize too that your new opportunities may lead down unproductive paths. Some men fantasize an image of the eligible man as being sexually active, hard drinking, enjoying multiple female relationships, and treating life casually. Few men adopt this life style, and none lead it for long.

Being single can have its drawbacks and problems. Friends may insist upon taking sides with you or your ex-wife and may either snub you or try to draw you into disparaging her. Couple-oriented activities become uncomfortable, and some old friendships just die.

You will have to decide what friendships you would like to continue and how to keep these relationships healthy. Also, you have excellent opportunities now to broaden your friendships. Thus, you may decide on the kinds of new relationships you want to develop and how soon. Considerations on when and how your children will be drawn into these new relationships will also be made.

A SPECIAL DIMENSION: TIME

The important effects of time have become one of the distinguishing characteristics of twentieth-century science. Both the physical and social sciences now employ dynamic models to explain events; the timing of interactions must be understood before describing how they will interact. A divorce has three important time effects. A good way to think about them is as time past, time present, and time future.

Time Past. Everyone has memories to deal with: family relationships, your first love, high-school friends, further schooling, moving away from your family, and your first full-time job. Others pertain more directly to your family: courting and marriage, your first child, birthday parties, when you taught your children to ride a two-wheeler, the excitement of Christmas, and trips to relatives'. Memories.

Some of these memories are good to retain: those that confirm that your past was happy, that you are a good person, and that others love and appreciate you. Some memories stand in the way of your growth by fixating your thoughts on the past; by eliciting anger, sadness, or guilt; and by placing roadblocks to growth and development in your way.

Time past is bound to play a strong part in your life. You have some control over how past events are used. Many men find professional counseling helpful in sorting out the past while constructing a healthy present time orientation.

Time Present. Perhaps the greatest potency of the effect of time is seen in life's repetitiveness. The days, weeks, months, and seasons recur in routine cycles which provide a stable foundation for our lives. Divorce is so difficult, in part, because daily routines are disrupted. Recovery comes when a comfortable balance of the routine and the novel is re-established; when there is a sense of knowing what today, or this week, or this year, is likely to bring.

Family rituals such as birthdays and holidays represent a sense of stability and require special attention. Many people want to avoid them for awhile or to celebrate them in totally new ways. You should realize, however, that children generally want to emphasize the routine and familiar. The present time should be used to create and maintain wholesome stability and consistency in their lives. Through consistent and regular routines, children gain control and understanding of their world and anticipate the future with greater confidence. Be aware that fathers who do not celebrate and acknowledge special days and events may be excluded later by their children from participating in them.

Time Future. This dimension can ring with a sense of excitement and hopefulness or of stagnation and depression. Your thoughts and feelings about the directions your life is taking become a good barometer of your mental health. Having a good feeling about your future becomes the cornerstone of the rebuilding process. Resolving this sense of time means that you have completed the restoration process and the picture is whole again.

Your Children and Time

Children also have these senses of time past, present, and future, but they may not use them all at once. As we will see later, the children's ages and their concepts of time affect their responses to a divorce.

For example, preschoolers understand the time present and the routine aspects of life. Research indicates that a disruption of stable routines causes the most difficulty for them after their parents divorce. By building predictability into their young children's lives and making daily activities and visiting schedules clear, parents minimize the children's trauma.

Children of elementary school age with divorcing parents tend to focus on time past—the way the family used to be as a "regular" and whole family. They get involved in remembering how time at holidays and summers was spent and the daily morning-to-night family routine when both Mom and Dad lived with them. Issues of divided loyalty between their parents or the loss of a less-frequently-present parent emerge.

Junior-high-school-age children begin to think in terms of time future. They begin to consider and develop their goals for families and look at their own family as a model to see how well it compares to others. They are apt to become very angry, even to withdraw, if they judge their parents to be failures. By withdrawing, they deny being associated with parents who are inadequate in achieving suitable goals for family life.

These illustrations point out that your children's perceptions of the divorce will differ from yours. They are not trying to reconstruct a picture nor starting over. They are just starting. They are trying to construct a picture of themselves, you, their mother, and a family, from scratch. Remember that your decisions have a strong bearing on how they form and frame their picture. Hopefully, you will choose to remain an active and supportive father. They need you. Moreover, you need them.

Summary

Reading this may be somewhat discouraging. Divorce is not a simple or easy process. The experiences of other divorced men clearly show that divorce is a period of transitions. The picture will be put back together again, but reconstruction takes time and energy. Most divorced men do it, and often end up with a picture that is better than the one left behind. A key is to keep the whole picture in mind while working on small parts of it at a time. Make your own decisions about how you want the finished picture to look, and keep adjusting your strategies to make it become a reality.

2

Your Psychological and Social Changes

Thomas Oakland

Over two million men in this country are becoming or recently have been divorced. In some cases, a divorce is a welcome goal following years of turmoil. For most, however, divorce is an unwelcome event—a seemingly unavoidable tragedy. Both partners may have judged the relationship to be beyond repair; yet, many men actively or passively oppose a divorce. While aware of the stresses in their marriage, they often do not want a divorce and are unprepared to accept fully the many changes they initially experience.

Yet, these men invariably make the transition from marriage through a divorce—a transition marked by four broad passages.

PASSAGES THROUGH DIVORCE

Deciding to Divorce

Think back to the beginning of your relationship with your former wife; when you met, dated, got engaged, and married. This formation took months, perhaps years. Recall, too, the time since then while you established a family, home, career, friends, and many other dimensions of your life. Relationships require much communication time if they are to mesh and engage properly. Their disengagement also requires communication and time.

The husband or wife who suddenly packs his or her bags, moves out, and employs a lawyer to handle all legal responsibilities, sets in motion a process likely to cause severe damage to him- or herself and the family.

Consider the opposite extreme: the possibility of divorce that has been considered for years. A marriage may be unrewarding but is maintained because of the children, financial considerations, family or religious pressures, or a hundred other reasons. Given this situation, one or both partners will likely spend little time with their family, and even less time in intimate relationships with their spouse, and more time at work or in establishing stronger relationships with friends and companions of either sex. Progress toward a divorce is slow and steady. Mutual unhappiness is recognized and discussed, but the real reasons may be avoided. While the partners may have sincerely tried to resolve their problems some time ago, one or both now have given up and are resigned to accept their marriage as unfulfilling.

Once a decision to divorce is made, however, a husband and wife need ample time alone to discuss the many issues they both face. Some issues involving both persons include living arrangements before the divorce, the continued use of the home or apartment, disposition of other property, continued financial arrangements, and informing relatives and friends. Of course, a multitude of issues surrounding the children also need the attention of both. Issues which involve only one spouse may be handled alone.

Discussions at this time should also include matters of an even more personal nature. A couple's relationship—the thoughts, feelings, and behaviors they had and have for one another—should be examined. Couples need to discuss why a divorce is occurring. While the temptation to criticize and cut down one's partner may be strong, this unbalanced approach can cause irreparable damage and pain. Also, the need to rescue one another from the pain and anguish each may be experiencing should be explored. Recognize the mutual need to understand what went well and what went wrong in the relationship.

Marriage is the most intimate and intense relationship people ever experience. Couples often think they know one another before marriage only to discover after marriage that their prior understanding was shallow and incomplete. Both the man and woman going through a divorce can gain valuable information and insights about themselves and how they function in relationships if both are willing to talk and listen. Most adults need to know how they are seen by their partner and to inform their partner about how they feel and think toward them now.

Communication among many couples is strong and productive at this time. In fact, many surprisingly rediscover the rewards of open and meaningful discussions. They often are able to identify points on which both agree or disagree and to try to understand the other's point of view. Emphasis should be placed on describing feelings, thoughts, and actions instead of evaluating them as good or bad. The atmosphere should allow each to accept those points which seem correct and to put aside those which seem wrong. Wild accusations and sarcastic evaluations should be avoided since they only add to the difficulties.

Divorce often occurs in an atmosphere of love. Most people seeking a divorce still have feelings of affection and care. These can be expressed at this time through the ways partners communicate with and act toward each other.

Time, in addition to communication, is another important factor affecting separation and divorce. A coming-together period extends over months, sometimes years. The disengagement period also should occur over time.

Strive to promote understanding of yourself and each other. You need an opportunity to put your life in order. Telling the children, finding new living quarters, buying furniture (and other necessary items), preparing for financial and legal changes, and a myriad of other responsibilities cannot be rushed. Consider, too, that divorce-related stresses may deplete your energy and stamina. Don't expect to accomplish all that you set for yourself each day.

Time with one another is also needed. Communicating takes time. Various issues need discussion. Moreover, you probably will need to discuss some issues many times. Don't be surprised if your divorce-related discussions take three to six months. Consider this an opportunity to disengage in a healthy and beneficial fashion.

Time for yourself is also needed. All people need periods of solitude to think about various matters. Some find solitude in walking, in reading, in the quiet of a church or park, in a favorite room, or with a receptive, non-judgmental friend. Some seek solitude through drinking or drugs; these however, cloud thoughts and may contribute to depression at a time when the positive qualities are needed. Don't consider periods while driving or doing other competing activities as part of this time for yourself. Set aside one or more hours daily to allow an uninterrupted consideration of a few key problems.

This first passage for many men is a time of grief. The hopes and dreams they had for themselves and their family seem broken and destroyed. Some men are able to cry and to express grief in therapeutic ways. Others find this difficult and attempt to deal with their sadness in other ways.

For example, they first may deny they have any problems. Their words and behavior attempt to mask the difficulties they find in adjusting to their new life. To admit to problems may be seen as a sign of weakness.

This false front can be maintained for only so long. Their denial may turn to anger. Their anger may be directed either toward themselves or others. Inwardly-directed anger is seen when men try to punish themselves physically (through suicide or other forms of self-destructive behaviors), psychologically (through self-derogatory comments), or socially (through withdrawing from others). Some exhibit self-annihilation tendencies by also renouncing their commitment to vocational and financial obligations.

Family members and friends often are the objects for externally directed anger. Verbal abuse by phone or face to face, uninvited visits which end in physical assaults, and legally-imposed restraining orders often form a sequence of events which reflect the frustration and anger some men feel.

Anger usually is used in an attempt to resolve conflicts. It rarely succeeds. Realizing its severe limitations, other strategies such as bargaining, assertiveness, or acceptance may be used.

Bargaining involves communicating in ways which enable compromises to be made. The intent is for all parties to succeed while minimizing their losses. Bargaining and compromising between a man and his spouse prior to and during the divorce hopefully may lead to their being able to talk about and compromise on certain issues after the divorce. As much as most men may try, they rarely find themselves totally freed from all relationships with their former wives. This is particularly true when children are involved.

During this first passage, communicating, bargaining, and compromising are difficult. You may feel that you are being pushed out of your home, deprived of your children, robbed of income, and whiplashed by an acrimonious divorce proceeding. Cordial relationships with your former wife may be difficult, near impossible to establish, and your feelings border on the vengeful, hating, and destructive.

Men with more moderate feelings, who see the need to be civil and to seek compromises their wives, may face cold resistance and uncompromising attitudes.

At this point, men often realize how little power and authority they have. The courts and their wives seem to have constructured a strong, high, narrow fence about them which severely restricts what they are allowed to do. Fairness no longer is considered. Try as they may, man may not be able to seek a proper solution to their concerns and grievances.

Examples are numerous. Children have freer access to their neighbors than to a noncustodial father. Children are even restricted from phoning him. Mothers may refuse to acknowledge legitimate visitation rights. Fathers who see child support payment frivolously spent on tobacco, liquor, and a mother's personal clothing, must continue to send money or face the possibility of being jailed.

These problems, plus others, often lead to severe mental depression during the first year. Men often see no way out of their dilemma. They also are prone to physical illnesses, real or psychosomatic.

Disengagement, Distress and Disorientation

Most men find divorce a serious shock to their lives. Disruptions occur on all fronts: socially, emotionally, financially, and vocationally. Men go from a somewhat orderly life to one where new life styles must be established. They face an onrush of decisions, changes, and challenges. Taking them one at a time, men can cope; faced with them all at once, many men do not do well.

Over the years, common goals, commitments, customs, habits, and laws established directions for life. A divorce dissolves many of these life directions.

What took years to put together cannot be displaced overnight. During the disengagement process, men must learn to live apart from their former wives and most likely their children, other family members, friends, and neighbors. They often find life lonely. While they grew and lived as members of many groups, they now are excluded from membership in some. They are forced to become more independent and self-sufficient.

Life during this second passage has few pre-established directions. Thus, there are countless ways to use time and resources and to respond to daily responsibilities. Some men during this period choose life styles which do not promote their adjustment, while others, through good judgement and luck, develop healthier living patterns.

Unhealthy Adjustment Patterns.   Some men face divorce by withdrawing and becoming detached from activities and people who gave them happiness. For some men, divorce is both painful and humiliating. By retreating they think their wounds will be salved and their humiliation lessened. Men who withdraw often expect friends and loved ones to come to their rescue. Disappointment grows into bitterness when their expectations go unmet.

Withdrawal may be coupled with an increase in alcoholic consumption. One or two drinks after work become a routine and then a starting point for even greater consumption. The Friday Happy Hour which provided a welcome change in the week's calendar can become a nightly search for affiliation and withdrawal from a multitude of stressful personal situations. Drug consumption, both prescribed and illegal, can serve the same purpose. Being under the influence may be used as a license for physically injuring themselves and others. Anger often is vehemently expressed toward a former spouse, family members or friends while they are drunk. Though seemingly restful and soothing, excessive alcohol and drug consumption is expensive, abuses one's mind and body, and limits one's ability to meet and handle responsibilities successfully.

Some men find new women entering their lives who provide understanding, compassion, and love at a time when these needs are not met by others. That new relationships seemingly are more rewarding and important than older ones is used to justify pulling away from family and friends further.

Some men find one or two women entering their lives while others are intent upon living a fantasy filled by scores of women. Some describe this as a man's second adolescence. The hurt and rejection following a divorce for some men is translated into a compelling need to prove their masculinity through sexual attraction and prowess. New moral codes partially erase a double standard and now allow women to engage more openly and freely in various sexual relationships. Women are more available sexually and often initiate social and sexual relationships. Men's clothing, eating, sleeping, and grooming patterns may change to support this new image.

Men may develop significant medical problems in the face of hardships and defeats. They may put on weight, exercise less, eat an unbalanced diet, sleep irregularly, and drink and smoke heavily. These and other factors exacerbate existing medical problems. A few develop new and serious coronary problems, including strokes, as a way to free themselves from responsibilities and defeats. Less chronic and severe illnesses like colds and the flu seem to linger longer. Men may be more likely to miss work. Psychosomatic illnesses flourish. A variety of debilitating emotions—anger, fear, depression and loneliness—seem to accompany debilitating medical conditions. Severe debilitating conditions in one area are likely to trigger those in other areas.

While divorce often brings economic hardships, some men have more spendable income or choose to live more heavily on credit, thus allowing themselves to spend their way to happiness. The rental or purchase of a modish apartment complete with a wet bar and view, a new car (preferably a sporty foreign convertible), and seasonal vacations distract some men from the gloomy side of life and project an image of an avant-garde and successful person. Fun-filled weekends with the children, good restaurants, and expensive shopping trips are but a few ways fathers attempt to impress their children, and perhaps attempt to punish their former wives. A visible mark of a man's success comes with his financial success. Thus, while some men choose liquor, drugs or sex as their opiates, others find spending money a temporary key to happiness during this second phase.

No society has more freedoms and fewer restrictions than ours. Traditional sources for developing and maintaining moral and ethical conduct (such as churches, small and intimate neighborhoods, extended and close family units, and local, state, and federal governments) have lost much of their influence. Traditional standards establishing right from wrong have been transformed in the wake of a pluralistic society which emphasizes relative values. For some, this is a license to live any kind of life since there are no rights or wrongs. The essence of life lies in its discoveries. Anything goes.

Thus, for some men, this second phase marked by disengagement, distress, and disorientation is filled with a series of unhealthy adjustment patterns. Their paths lead to culs-de-sac and dead ends. Others, however, develop healthier adjustment patterns during this first year. While facing the same sources of distress and anguish, they make some wise choices which place them in healthier trajectories.

Healthy Adjustment Patterns. We find help and support from many areas in our life. Our immediate family, an extended family (of uncles, aunts, and cousins), neighbors and friends, involvement in community affairs (church, scouting, or political groups, unions, fraternal societies), sports (as a participant, a coach, or a spectator), hobbies, arts and crafts, the stock market and other forms of investing, and refinishing furniture or an old car are but some areas from which people derive pleasure. Some of these support systems involve activities; others involve people; some involve both. Maintaining involvement in these life-supporting systems helps to insure a healthy social and emotional transition through this first year or two.

The old saying, "We don't know the value of water until the well runs dry," applies to many areas, especially to physical well-being. Most take their health for granted. Yet, when physical problems arise, they may realize that their social, emotional, and financial well-being may be related to their physical well-being. By anticipating the tendency for physical ailments to increase during this second passage, you have taken the first important step toward preventing illnesses. Proper eating and sleeping patterns are necessary to stay healthy and well energized.

Some days, everything seems to go wrong. If this becomes somewhat habitual, see if there is a reasonable explanation for this pattern. Some days seem to be keyed to how they start. Waking up late (and perhaps tired), rushing through a shower and dressing, arguing with the children, running into heavy traffic, forgetting some important papers at home, and arriving conspicuously late to work are no way to begin your day. Similar stressful events can occur toward the end of one's day and prevent a restful sleep. Attempt to start and end each day calmly. Plan ahead so as to allow sufficient time for all known responsibilities plus a little cushion for some unforeseen emergencies.

Set realistic goals for each day and concentrate on completing them. Using problem-solving strategies to tackle high priority concerns successfully encourages progress toward resolving problems and finding greater happiness.

Have some goals toward which to work. Don't lack direction. The story is told of an envious neighbor who asked a farmer how his crops were always formed in perfectly straight rows. The farmer replied that he kept his eye on and drove straight toward a distant point while planting. The suggestion to work toward the future may be difficult to accept when life's daily activities seem to be in disarray. Future plans seem shattered. Depression, distress, and disorientation characteristic of this second passage are testimony to the lack of confidence you may have in your future. Depression lingers longer among persons who lack goals toward which to work.

You may start by thinking of your future as next weekend. Decide on some goal, work toward it a bit daily, and reward yourself if it is reached (and deny yourself the reward if it is not). Asking someone for a date, calling an old friend, learning how to prepare that French sauce you love, looking at guitars, buying a new novel, or cleaning your golf clubs are activities in pursuit of larger and long-term goals. At this point keep one or two long-term goals in mind and work toward them regularly. You will alter these goals as others become more attractive.

Many goals are not achieved. Problem-solving strategies may not succeed. In fact, there is no simple set of rules to follow which allows you to pull yourself out of this by your own boot straps. Recognize that all people going through a divorce need help, particularly during this second phase. To not ask for help or to refuse it when offered serves to extend the length of this most difficult period.

An image exists that a strong, successful man never admits to a weakness nor asks for help. Some characterize this as *machismo*. Men adhering to this image as a model for their lives chase a mirage. No one is self-sufficient, and everyone needs help. To not ask for help does not remove the weakness but helps to insure its existence.

During this stage you tend to be especially sensitive to what others say about you. Their impact often is significant, but how sensitive are you to what you say about yourself? What you say to yourself about yourself (psychologists call this self-talk) may be more important than what others say about you. To say you are in constant communication with yourself sounds a bit silly. Yet, psychology is just beginning to understand how self-talk strongly influences your feelings and actions. However, positive self-talk can produce significant improvements in self-esteem and actions.

The self-talk of some people clearly is negative and may be seen in their attitudes and behaviors. The person who tells himself, "I'm fat and unattractive; nobody likes me, and I can understand why," is creating an image that can become a self-fulfilling prophecy. He is likely to feel and act like a fat and unattractive person who few people like. Conversely, the person who tells himself, "I am good looking, and people generally like me," is likely to feel and act accordingly. In fact, those comments came from the same person, the first before and the second following professional help. His attitude and self-talk, not his physical appearance, changed.

The discussion of adolescent characteristics indicates that how adolescents evaluate their own bodies is more important than an objective appraisal of their physique. Adults also use subjective judgements to form self-images which become translated into communication patterns that strongly effect thoughts and actions.

Men successful during this second phase tend to generate positive self-talk statements which create an image that becomes self-fulfilling. Those who think "I'm O.K.," tend to be thought of as being O.K. Conversely, those who have prolonged despair and depression tend to think negatively about themselves. An attitude "I'm not O.K.," often is proof that people are their own sharpest critics.

Progress through this stage also is furthered by minimizing other major or sudden changes in your life. Difficulties in dealing with divorce-related problems are great enough at this time. Don't invite other stress producers into your life now.

Many men see a post-divorce period as the chance to begin a new life. The old one seems so bad that major changes appear warranted on every side. Men believing this may change employers and professions, give up long-term friendships, move out of state, seek a flashy and tinseled image, and make other significant alterations in their lives. Contrary to their intent, they are likely to compound divorce related problems, increase their instability, and prolong their adjustment. Adults never can start anew—only babies can. However, deliberate and steady progress toward self-improvement is possible and is to be encouraged. Successful readjustment involving one major area of life is increased by maintaining constancy and stability in other areas. Minimizing other major or sudden changes also allows men to maintain more stable relationships with their children, a quality they need at this time.

Finally, men who rebound well during this first year tend to concentrate their attention and energy on doing their best each day and not to dissipate their abilities by worrying about the future.

Life before the divorce was full. Fathers now may find additional responsibilities somewhat overwhelming. Work, home, family, and personal responsibilities require daily attention.

Attend to them first by assessing their relative importance. Consider how you use your time. Do you devote most of your time to what is most important or to trivia? By making your bed, shopping each day, not allowing the children to wear their jeans a second day, cooking separate meals, spending a lot of free time making new acquaintances, responding to all requests, feeling guilty if the sports page is not read, and worrying about and doing hundreds of other low-priority activities, you waste your time and energies. At night you correctly question what you accomplished that day.

Successful companies have plans which guide their daily work; unsuccessful ones have no plans. Yet, the successful companies do not always follow their exact plans. Success depends on recognizing your most important responsibilities, providing sufficient time for them, sticking generally to the game plan, allowing for the unexpected though important, and putting aside those activities that really do not matter. Many men put a 3 x 5 card in their shirt pocket daily as a reminder of their priorities. Each night it is reviewed and a new one prepared for the following day.

Concentration on doing well today encourages continuous adjustment and decreases the likelihood of becoming overwhelmed by anxiety and depression. We feel more confident about our future when we are pleased with each day's activities. By accomplishing important goals each day, we feel in control of our lives and confidently approach larger responsibilities.

Orientation and Integration

During the pre-divorce period, you often face the question, "What is happening to me?" You feel victimized and experience a severe loss of control. Then during the first year or two following the divorce, you may wonder, "How can I best cope?" You seek changes which provide meaning to your life. Finally during the third stage, which often emerges during the third or fourth year, after divorce, you commonly seek an answer to the question, "Who am I?" With a growing sense of identity and direction, your life increasingly reflects healthy orientations and greater integration.

Prior to this time, being divorced has largely had negative connotations, and the burdens and difficulties of life overshadowed any advantages of being single. However, the advantages of being single and being able to exercise more control over events are recognized more clearly now. You can handle basic domestic responsibilities routinely. Shopping and food preparation, laundry, and other household tasks somehow get done. Relationships with the children have almost evened out. Visitation schedules, school-related matters, clothes purchases, and other aspects associated with readjustment generally are going well. Life is more orderly and stable. There may even be a greater closeness between you and your children now than there was before the divorce.

During this period, you may also experience a renewed interest in and commitment to your work. Some men quite honestly are not fully involved in their work during the first two stages. Their thoughts are distracted, their time is consumed by personal matters, and their energies are directed toward other priorities or dissipated through stress and anxiety. But now that your personal life is more rewarding and orderly, you can allow yourself greater involvement in your work. This growing sense of direction makes the future look brighter and exciting. Some men even become unusually creative and productive. Experimenting with and discovering new dimensions to their personal lives often encourages them to think and act more creatively at work. The old ways are not necessarily seen any more as the only or best ways of handling responsibilities. Being able to live a different life successfully outside of work tends to encourage men to seek new and better solutions to problems at work.

Though finances may remain a problem, legal fees have usually by now been paid off as have the big bills associated with establishing a new home. You have learned to live within your income. Except for inflation, finances no longer remain a number one problem.

Those of you who enter this third stage and go beyond are often able to develop a balanced life style with a healthy mixture of personal and vocational pursuits, social involvements, personal time, and continuous relationships with family and friends. No one area completely overshadows another. Degrees of enjoyment are found in all.

How you have come to think about your personal qualities and those of others is the key to successful passage through this stage. During this integration phase, men are able to chuck hatred and animosity they may hold toward their former mates and instead to accept their new roles. Hate and animosity are debilitating emotions which inflect greater harm on the bearer than the intended victim. Being free of hatred and animosity now allows men to establish new and healthier relationships with women in general as well as with their former mates.

Knowing how to use lessons from a former marriage creatively often is difficult. You cannot deny its existence. Thus, how can it be used constructively?

During this stage men often learn to remember the good times and enriching events as proof of their good qualities. The celebration of special events (your wedding, the birth of children, promotions at work) and holidays, vacations, the purchase of your first house are but some of the big events which you may remember with fondness. The smaller events also provide many nice memories: the children participating in their first Christmas program, presenting a very special gift to your former wife, a summer evening spent in the park, the times you laughed together at funny movies, or cried together because of sadness. Those memories cannot and should not be put aside. Rather they form the ingredients for reconstructing a positive, well-balanced, and wholesome life. By remembering and emphasizing the good times and enriching events, you create positive expectation regarding your future and a positive attitude toward yourself and others, thus furthering the reconstruction process.

Consolidation and Continuity

This last stage is reached when you see divorce as one of life's important milestones, one of many events helping to shape the course of life. Prior to this time, the effects and implications of divorce have loomed large, invading all segments of life, and seemingly controlling all events.

Some men try a second marriage during the first stage, often with someone with whom they work or a family friend, but these relations usually do not work out. Both parties soon separate with disappointment and bitterness.

During the second stage men often seek marriage in order to take care of them and perhaps of their children. The major question during this stage, "How can I cope," is answered by finding someone who provides a home for you. At this stage you often have experienced little personal growth and are likely to choose a mate who is similar to the one you have just left. You also are likely to experience problems similar to those encountered in the first marriage.

During the third stage the divorced man is still experiencing growth and self-discovery. Thus, his attitudes and behaviors often are irregular and inconsistent. Marriage at this time may thwart further necessary growth.

During the fourth stage men are more confident of themselves and others. They know and accept their strengths and weaknesses while allowing the same for others. They are able to form healthy interrelationships, able to share, to give, and to receive. They generally feel secure about themselves and can trust and love others. They also are able to seek a healthy and stable relationship with another partner. For many, marriage is in order. Men who come through the first three stages are likely to possess the personal qualities necessary for a successful marriage.

Remarriage. That someone so hurt by a divorce would seek another relationship which too may end that way seems somewhat strange, but in fact most people who divorce do not give up on marriage. They divorce because the relationships did not live up to their idea of what marriage should be. Most divorced men are likely to marry again, because few men find adequate substitutes to a monogamous life style. Men who live with different women rarely view nonmarital cohabitation as an acceptable substitute for marriage.

Your chances for happiness the second time around are very good. Persons who remarry tend to be as happy as those who remain in their first marriage. This occurs despite the fact that many remarriages are plagued with financial problems or conflicts between stepparent and stepchild (particularly, between stepmothers and stepdaughters).

Steps toward a successful marriage begin with the women you date. By being selective at this point, you are more likely to choose a mate with whom you will be happily married.

While there are no guarantees for success, women who have certain qualities are more able to enter into and sustain a loving relationship and work cooperatively toward a successful marriage. Women who know and accept themselves are likely to be mature and settled in their life style. Choose someone whose life seems to have had positive themes rather than negative ones. A woman who has had a happy life, particularly a loving childhood, is likely to continue this happy and loving theme. Such a person is able both to give and to receive love and affection. A person who is liked by many people, one who has many good and extended friendships, is likely to exhibit good personal qualities. Of course, you want someone who is able to make and keep commitments and who places you and her relationship with you high in her priorities.

Be aware of various pitfalls to successful marriages. The following are but three of the more common ones which may compel a man to marry prematurely:

- Women may have an overpowering need to marry and may use various tactics to manipulate men toward marriage.

- Men may face intolerable pressures "to make a home" for the children. Parents, neighbors, and especially the courts often incorrectly view a single-parent house headed by a father as something less than a home.

- Confusing sex and love has been the downfall of many men. Many men seek a permanent relationship with someone who is sexually attractive only to discover the luster wearing off and the base material thin and tarnished.

Examine, too, your own characteristics. Hopefully, you will choose someone you consider your equal, someone with whom you find various conversations pleasant and extended. Your likes and dislikes should be similar. Contrary to popular belief, opposites don't attract and stay together very long. With the maturity which comes with age and experience, you should be able to describe your partner's assets and defects accurately and objectively and enter the relationship accepting her without intentions of changing her later.

The proverbial divorcee "marrying on the rebound" is likely to encounter a severely strained relationship. The rebound can occur because a man wants to show his former mate how attractive he is to other women. Other men seek a nurturing, mothering relationship from a woman who will take care of them during this time of need. Rebounds occur for a hundred different reasons, all of which can spell hardship.

Recognize, too, that remarriage is not necessary for all men. Some clearly lack the personal characteristics necessary for a successful marriage and wisely choose to remain single. Others have the personal characteristics for a successful remarriage and choose to develop a personal life style in which quality friendships and companionships meet their social needs. Our society truly is pluralistic and offers men an opportunity to choose among various healthy life styles. Remarriage is only one of many options.

Meeting Your Needs

One goal of life should be the ability to function effectively and happily as a total person. This implies that you are in control of your thoughts, feelings, and actions and that you generally approve of them. Moreover, you are aware of and respond favorably to others. The healthy person strives to resolve rather than prolong conflicts when they arise.

The discussion of children's development identifies ten basic needs which must be met in order for them to be healthy. The healthy adult also has basic needs which must be met. A person's mental health largely depends on the degree to which his basic needs are met and how they are met. These needs constitute guideposts toward a healthy living style. Thus, their importance must be underscored at this time.

Close Physical Contact. Being deprived of close physical contact is one of the most difficult experiences of divorce. Many men have enjoyed rewarding sexual experiences with their former wives. Moreover, there is a real security and comfort derived through snuggling, touching, and just lying physically close to someone else. Close physical contact carries a psychological message which translates into "I'm O.K., you're O.K." By being deprived in this area, you may come to think that you are not O.K., that you are unlovable as well as unloved.

Positive Evaluations from Important Others. Being ostracized, forgotten, or ignored can be the most devastating form of punishment. These and other forms of rejection seem to cluster during a divorce. Men often sense their immediate and extended families drawing away, their friends being unresponsive, and their co-workers busily engaged in their own lives and not really caring. Recognition and attention is particularly strong at this time. The need to receive compliments from those they like and admire reassures them that they are good and capable.

Feeling of Competence. Some days everything seems to go wrong. Your favorite clothes are dirty, the car develops problems on the way to work, and the important project due soon at the office is behind schedule. Your boss may draw this and other problems to your attention, and even bring up your secret thought that perhaps you are not capable of doing the job. And this comes on the heels of accusations that the divorce is due to your incompetence.

Most men enjoy work because of its challenges. Although money is important, we also work because of a commitment to do a good job. The feeling of competence you strive for at work also can be nurtured at home. You can feel good about being a good father, a good gardener, a good golfer—taking pride in various roles and activities. Everyone needs to know he is successful.

Assistance in Overcoming and Solving Problems.   Boys often are raised to be strong by being independent, by facing problems squarely, and by solving them alone. Many men continue to hold onto this attitude. For them, strength lies in their stoic independence. Asking for help shows signs of weakness. Many of these same men will later show severe signs of stress by developing heart trouble, cerebral hemmorhages and strokes, and psychotic breakdowns.

People never have been able to solve all their problems alone. Mankind came together, formed communities and families in recognition of this mutual interdependence. We all have needs which we cannot meet alone. We often need help in solving problems. In fact our strength often lies in taking advantage of the help and advice of knowledgeable and trusted advisors.

For most men, divorce is a new experience—a confusing, depressing, bewildering, complexing time. Because they lack the experience and knowledge, they should turn to others who can provide help to solve some of the major problems they now face. Seeking assistance is a sign of good judgment.

Rules to Reduce Uncertainty.   For some men divorce is a signal that the old way does not work, that the rules they tried to live by do not lead to happiness and success. Their search for the right set of rules and values now may take many forms. Some look around only to find a bewildering number of life styles and values. Instead of discovering a new set of rules and values which seem to work for others, they throw up their hands in despair and conclude that anything goes. Divorce for these men is a time of abandonment. Their lives come to resemble a hot-air balloon in which one's elevation can be controlled but one's direction is determined by the prevailing winds. Life is directionless without a rudder.

Some men who reassess their rules and values discover the old ones, with slight modifications, remain applicable. Other men form a commitment to somewhat different rules and values. In both situations a renewed sense of direction and source of motivation emerge.

Rules reduce uncertainty by helping us develop habits to respond to every day events. Knowing the rules and establishing values encourages us to feel more confident in ourselves and in others. Life becomes more orderly.

Control over Your Life.   Some of the most frightening times occur when you feel out of control. Persons who have driven on ice or snow know the sensation of a car spinning helplessly. Attempts to control its direction by turning or breaking seem ineffective.

Life may sometimes resemble a spinning car, particularly during and soon after a divorce. Attempts to influence the outcome seem beyond control. Control over your life often rests with lawyers, judges, real estate agents, and your former wife. You are unable to fight the system.

The need for self-determination remains strong in each person. Your happiness depends upon your being able to determine how to utilize your time, talents, and resources. Learning how to be constructively assertive helps you regain control of your life while not intruding on the lives of others.

Balancing Autonomy and Affiliation.   One major theme emerging from this discussion of basic needs emphasizes self-actualization and self-development. Men have a need to receive praise and recognition for what they do, to know themselves, and to have self-control. These characteristics reflect a man's independence, his autonomy from others. A complementary theme also emerges that emphasizes a man's need to develop as a member of groups. Your happiness often depends upon feeling that you are an important part of groups whose members have common experiences, goals, and thus affiliations with you.

Man is a social animal and needs to be with others. This need grows out of the broader need for stability. Affiliating with others promotes the development of strong attachments which create a stable and regulated life.

Adjustment during a divorce is improved by maintaining many strong attachments with groups providing affiliation. Families constitute the most important source of affiliation. Thus, maintaining your involvement with your family is very important. Affiliations with other groups also are important. Churches, fraternal orders, sporting and card clubs, and musical groups are but a few of the numerous associations through which men acquire affiliations. Don't dissolve these during troubled times. Instead, draw upon them as a source of strength and stability.

Stimulation.   Men's minds, feelings, and bodies need to be energized and stimulated. Our minds and emotions are not like a passive computer, patiently waiting for some input to arrive. Rather, our senses seek out and need stimulation and arousal to remain alive. A proper balance in intellectual, emotional, and physical stimulation is needed to maintain a healthy life.

During and shortly after divorce, men face an overwhelming amount of stimulation. They may tend to be overstimulated (even overwhelmed) in certain areas—particularly emotional and intellectual— but at the same time be understimulated physically. Their major task lies in sorting out the stimuli, arranging them according to priorities, and responding to those which are most important.

Following the divorce, men may withdraw and retreat from normal activities, thus decreasing their intellectual, emotional, and physical stimulation. Prolonged understimulation leads to atrophy, a wasting away from the lack of nourishment.

During and following divorce men should monitor the amount of stimulation they face, striving to avoid both over- and understimulation.

Congruence.   People who experience congruence are said to be reliable and have integrity. Man has a need to be honest to himself and to others. Honesty to himself is apparent when his thoughts, feelings, words, and actions are consistent. For example, a father is congruent when his thoughts regarding how he wants to act toward his children are consistent with how he feels toward them as well as how he actually behaves toward them.

Congruence also is shown when a person is honest with others. His thoughts and feelings, if expressed to others, are accurate and consistent from person to person.

A divorce promotes incongruence. Thoughts and feelings fluctuate and may remain unstable for some time. Behavior also shows disorganization, and your thoughts, feelings, words, and actions toward your former spouse provide prime examples of this incongruence. Your thoughts about her may be quite negative; yet, your feelings toward her may vary from love to hate. You intend to say one thing but something quite different comes out. Actions toward her may range from friendly to cordial or simply wanting to avoid confrontation.

With time men tend to resolve the incongruences which come with divorce and return to a life style in which their thoughts, feelings, and actions are consistent. This marks an important milestone of their recovery from this difficult period.

However, many men discover problems which remain unsolved and basic needs which go unmet. Professional help may be required to overcome some problems and to promote change in certain areas. Getting professional help for you or your children may be the most effective way to resolve difficulties.

Getting Professional Help for You and Your Children

Knowing when to seek professional help to overcome problems is important. A few people successfully weather the storms associated with divorce alone and do not need professional help, but most need and could benefit from some kind of help during this time. One mark of maturity is to know your limitations and to seek help when needed.

Seek help when the following conditions exist:

- Basic psychological and social needs are not being met.
- Alternative ways to deal with conflicts are not apparent.
- Behavior is destructive toward one's self or others.

- There are few friends or trusted relatives in whom to confide and seek advice.
- Multiple problems appear which seem to have no solutions.
- You are unable to sort out priorities and maintain a commitment to goals.
- There is a persistent change in eating and sleeping patterns.
- One's peers or superiors suggest the need of professional attention.

Selecting a Professional. Selecting professional help can be treacherous. You are placing great trust in another. Thus, you want to know the person has the personal and professional qualities necessary to be of help to your or your children.

Some people mistakenly believe that problems can be handed over to a therapist who possesses magical powers to divine a way out of life's maze. No therapist has these abilities. Effective therapy requires the client to be an active participant, accepting responsibilities for seeking solutions to problems under the guidance of a professional who is objective, knowledgeable, and experienced in helping others through similar difficulties. No legitimate therapist offers a guarantee of success or a money-back offer. Yet, thousands of fathers and their children have benefited from professional help. Their passages through the stages of divorce have been quicker and healthier.

Healthy skepticism is needed when selecting professional help in all areas. Many quacks are quick to offer help but lack the necessary training and experience.

Three major professional groups tend to offer the majority of services to people experiencing divorce. Psychiatrists perhaps are the best known because of their work with people experiencing severe and chronic problems. They first acquire an undergraduate degree and then are trained in medicine. After obtaining their medical degree they take advanced training in their area of psychiatric specialty. Their professional training can take 6 to 8 years or longer and usually ends with a series of oral and written examinations in their specialty. Their strong background in the biological sciences and medicine tends to make them preferred professionals when psychological problems have a biological or chemical basis and when treatment requires medication.

Clinical psychology is a relatively new area within psychology that has come into its own in the last 30 years. Clinical psychologists first acquire an undergraduate degree and then specialize by taking a PhD in psychology. This training takes 4 to 6 years and generally includes a one-year professional internship. They also write a dissertation and take oral and written examinations in their specialty. Their strong background in psychology tends to make them the preferred professionals when psychological problems are associated with personality or learning.

Social workers constitute a third group, perhaps the largest group of professionals trained to work with people in crisis. They, too, first acquire an undergraduate degree and then take a 2- or 3-year graduate program leading to a masters degree. Their training tends to be strongly oriented toward sociology and social psychology. Their strong background in group processes tends to make them the preferred professionals when various problems (such as social, financial, legal, and domestic) occur simultaneously within a family and there is the need for multiple kinds of services.

Other professional and nonprofessional groups also offer services. Some ministers, priests, and rabbis specialize in general counseling and welcome opportunities to be of service to families. Churches, associations for divorced persons (such as Parents Without Partners and Fathers for Equal Rights) frequently sponsor support groups. These typically meet weekly, are organized and led by people within the group, and are designed to provide mutual assistance to adults going through a divorce.

While differences exist in the training and experience of psychiatrists, psychologists, and social workers, the actual practices of professionals from all three groups are often similar. Consider the above information as guidelines in choosing the person best able to work with you or your children.

A special word of caution may be warranted in seeking help for children. More therapists are available to work with adults than with children. Moreover, therapies which are effective with adults often are not effective with children. Thus, be sure to select a therapist for children who has had sufficient training and experience with them.

In selecting a therapist, first recognize that each person or each family has unique sets of characteristics and problems. No one therapist will be effective for all people. Thus, you will need to interview three or four people who seem appropriate. Your interview with each professional will help you judge the degree of rapport you have and to gain some important information.

You will finally select someone who seems right for you, someone to whom you can relate well, whom you trust and have confidence in. Also, you will need answers to the following questions.

What degrees do they have, and what is the quality of their training? Have they recently completed continuing education programs on divorce-related problems? What was the focus during their internship, and what amount of training have they had with adults or children? These constitute some of the questions related to training.

Questions pertaining to practice are somewhat broader. How long is therapy likely to take? What is the cost and what payment plans must be followed? How long have they been in practice, do they specialize, and whom do they normally have as clients? What types of treatments or therapies are used? Do they prefer to work with clients individually, in groups, or in families? What are their attitudes toward medication? Are they available at other times if there is a crisis?

You may want to add other questions to your list. Though you may feel strange asking these questions, competent professionals recognize the importance of supplying this information and helping you select the right person likely to be of greatest benefit. Quite frankly, there are many quacks practicing in this area. You must get sufficient information to make sure the professional you choose is likely to help you and your children. Don't leave your decision to luck or good fortune.

3

Understanding Your Children

Thomas Oakland

Being a father is an exciting privilege. As a father you have
countless opportunities to observe significant changes occurring
rapidly over a few years and to see your children develop from fum-
bling neophytes to mature adults. More importantly, you play a
vital role in their lives, and influence their development in countless
ways. As providers, you help insure their physical needs are met.
You also provide by strongly influencing their thoughts, attitudes,
and behaviors. By providing opportunities and placing restrictions
on them, you help shape their growth in various ways.

You also are the beneficiaries of your children's actions. Years
ago children were valued as economic units, a form of cheap labor
to use by the family on the farm or in the shop. Fortunately, these
times are gone. We now can appreciate the vitality, inquisitiveness,
and love children possess and share. A reciprocal relationship
develops between healthy fathers and children in which basic
human needs are met.

Fathers have a reputation for not being very knowledgeable
when it comes to children. Men often are characterized as being
more involved with activities outside the home while women are
characterized as being more involved with activities within the

home. This characterization, though true for some families, is too simplistic and applies to fewer and fewer households. One half of all adult women are working now. Men increasingly are becoming more involved in child-rearing activities and in performing domestic chores. The reputation that men are not capable of raising children just is not true. Men can perform all activities important for raising children but two: bearing children and breast feeding.

THREE THEORIES OF BEHAVIOR

Understanding children requires a blend of theory and fact. This chapter discusses various theories and facts which pertain to children's development to provide a clear understanding of childhood.

There are three broad theories for describing and explaining behavior. One states that behavior is genetically determined; that is, our lives follow a path largely predetermined by the genes inherited from one's parents. This notion holds that there is little one can or should do to alter important life styles (except by controlling the gene pool through eugenics). Thus, because people can't change, the environment must be shaped to accommodate people. For example, some people believe that mental illness is a genetically determined trait which cannot be permanently altered. Thus, our society has created mental institutions which largely provide custodial care. This allows society to get the incurably insane off the street, yet allows them to live.

A second theory emphasizes the importance of environmental factors and discounts the importance of genetic contributions. The saying, "As the twig is bent, so grows the tree" is consistent with this idea. There is much we can do to shape important life styles. In fact, there are no limits to what we can do provided we have the will. Because people are infinitely flexible to adapt to all environments, little emphasis is placed on modifying environments. Thus, you will hear some people complain that schools do not adequately teach the basic skills to all children—that all children can learn to read if they had a quality education. People who hold an environment viewpoint believe that anything is possible given adequate resources.

A third idea, and the one most strongly held in the behavioral sciences, thinks of human behavior as a blend of genetic and environmental qualities. Your children will grow to resemble you physically. Children's height and weight, bone and teeth structure, visual and hearing acuity, and other physical features resemble their parents'. Less perceptible but no less real are intellectual, social, and emotional similarities. Thus, your contribution to your children starts at conception, but conception is just the start of life. Life's blueprint is not precisely mapped. While the genetic contributions are real and broadly define the boundaries in which behavior can occur, the environment also strongly influences how children develop.

Development may be characterized as a rock rolling down a mountain. At first, development is guided in a certain direction by a person's genetic make-up. However, its direction can be appreciably altered by giving it a shove before it gains strong momentum or by exerting a very strong force after it picks up speed. In both cases persistence and consistency help insure that a child's behavior follows the desirable course. Recognize, too, that other forces will exert their influences. Your efforts will be easier when other people in the child's life are pushing and nudging in the direction you want your child's lives to follow. Severe strains can occur when the efforts of others attempt to direct your child's life in opposite directions.

Thus, you cannot rule out the importance of genetic influences on children. However, your contribution to these influences lies behind you. Your attention should now be set on how the children's environment influences and molds their behavior now and in the future.

Another way of looking broadly at children is to consider their basic needs. All people have needs which must be met in order for them to survive. These needs are not restricted to childhood but comprise real needs which start early in life and continue until death. Thus, think of these as needs which both your children and you have.

Basic Needs

Courts award child support payments in order to insure that children's basic biological needs are met. Hopefully, you derive some satisfaction from knowing that your financial support helps to insure your children's basic biological needs are cared for when they are not with you. Responsibility for meeting these needs falls in your hands when your children are with you. Younger children require more careful planning and attention to insure their environment is safe, that proper nutrition is provided, and that they receive enough sleep. The importance of adequate rest and sleep should be underscored. Periods of rest and sleep allow the body to become repaired and rejuvenated and foster physical and mental health. Fathers who disregard children's normal sleeping hours by involving them in activities which conflict with naps or nighttime sleeping schedules often do them a disservice. Continued loss of sleep produces unlikeable, cranky, crabby children who are more susceptible to illness.

Greater challenges and rewards lie in your attempts to help children meet other basic needs, those of a social and psychological nature. Anyone can provide them financial support and thus meet their basic biological needs. A father's more personal form of providing is sharing his time and himself by being with his children. The following needs can be nurtured only in this personalized way.

Close Physical Contact

Children need to be held, caressed, touched, and to receive other forms of close physical contact. In our culture love is shared this way. Close physical contact is a form of communicating that "I'm OK and you're OK." Hugs and kisses throughout the day, your hand on their shoulder, and other forms of physical contacts are important.

Positive Evaluation from Important Others

All children yearn for compliments which also say, "You're OK." Children need assurance that you care enough about them to notice them, and what you notice about them you approve of. Positive comments from one's father are particularly welcome. Children recognize their importance and prize them above most anything else.

Feeling of Competence

We all need to take pride in a job well done. The toddler stumbling over to grandfather for the first time, the child riding a bike, the teenager receiving his first paycheck, the adult getting a promotion—all these say to the doer, "Well done." Though we cannot expect to do everything well, we do need the satisfaction of performing certain activities well. Positive evaluations from others and the feeling of competence are close allies. Your children need to hear positive comments from you and others when they do well. This encourages them to experience self-satisfaction, to pat themselves on the back at a job well done. The proverbial carrot continuously held out in front of the horse produces a frustrated, unhealthy animal. Your children need to know that you approve of some things they do.

Assistance in Overcoming and Solving Problems

Childhood is a time for acquiring skills for living. Many problems for children are astronomically large and formidable. They need help each day. The need for help to solve problems does not terminate after childhood. Adolescence adds other problems to the list—often of a social and emotional nature. In fact, potential problems seem to increase with age. Life becomes more complex. We never lose our need for help.

Become aware of problem areas your children have and let them know you are willing to help them. Your separation and divorce can create many disruptions in your children's lives—disruptions which pose new problems for them. Help them through the important regular problems of living plus new ones associated with the separation and divorce.

Rules to Help Define Good from Bad

Children need to be guided toward a set of beliefs which form the foundation for a good life. The characteristics cited as ideals by the Boy Scouts seem particularly noteworthy: trustworthy, loyal, helpful, friendly, courteous, kind, obedient, cheerful, thrifty, brave, clean, and reverent. The Ten Commandments and other sets of rules to live by help establish standards which enhance human life.

Some parents strive to not instill a set of rules and values in their children, preferring to let their children acquire them later. This attitude is unfortunate. It tends to instill confusion and disorder, to produce children who lack direction and are unable to distinguish right from wrong. Rules are needed to reduce uncertainties about what is appropriate behavior.

Discuss what you expect from your children when they are at home and when they are away. Consider establishing standards that are realistic, obtainable, and healthy. Your children, as they become older, should play a more active role in setting rules and guidelines for their own lives. Recognize, too, their rights to let you know what they expect from you. Be aware that your behavior sets an example to your children. Your most effective way to instill values in your children is to exhibit those qualities you want to see in them.

Sense of Control over Life

The need for control over our life is closely tied to the need for self-control and self-determination. Unfortunately, some people sense their lives being controlled and dominated by others. They experience frustration and anxiety when they recognize that the outcome of events is not influenced by what they do.

We experience a sense of control over our environment by recognizing different ways we can act, by accepting the consequences of our actions, and by seeing relationships between our actions and our outcomes. Gaining a sense of control over your life is easier if you know the rules and have them applied fairly and consistently. The next chapter identifies seven basic problem-solving stategies which, when used, also contribute to a sense of control.

Your children probably are experiencing a loss of self-control. The preschool children who cannot understand why mommy and daddy don't like one another, the 7- or 8-year-olds who soil their underwear, and the teenagers who shut themselves up in their rooms may be demonstrating their lack of control over important events shaping their lives. Gaining an understanding of what is happening to them and having knowledge of how they can shape their lives is important to your being able to help them adjust.

Balancing Affiliation and Autonomy

Man is a social animal. People of all ages have the need to feel a part of and to affiliate with one or more groups. Society has created groups to help foster our social, intellectual, and spiritual needs, and development occurs within these groups. However, development also occurs through self-actualization and through being somewhat independent, different, and autonomous from all others. For example, children should be encouraged to affiliate with and rely upon family, peers, schools, and other groups as sources of support but not to become totally dependent on any one group for their sustenance. A balance between group affiliation and individual pursuits is needed for proper growth and development.

Stimulation

Living is an active, growing process. Our body, mind, and spirit need nurturing and stimulation. We need to be activated, energized, aroused, and excited. We are stimulated by what is new, different, or intense; by people, places, events, and ideas.

Congruence

This perhaps is man's most basic psychological needs, and some find this very difficult to achieve. The need for congruence refers to the need for a unity among our thoughts, feelings, words, and actions. Others might describe this as honesty to one's self and to others.

Psychological and social problems are apparent in people whose thoughts, feelings, words, and actions are inconsistent and irregular. Children acquire congruence and honesty by having strong peer and adult models who display appropriate behaviors and expect congruence and honesty from them.

A Father's Role in Meeting Basic Needs

A child's environment rarely is neutral. It more often is charged with positive or negative qualities which serve to promote or impede development.

For example, some men after a divorce choose to fade away slowly, not to take an active part as a father. In reality, however, a father's retreat from his children has a negative impact on the children and himself. Inactivity is not neutral. Children's basic needs usually are not met under these circumstances. As a father, you can do much to insure your children's basic needs are met. Hopefully, you recognize that your responsibilities include and extend beyond basic biological needs which money often can provide. Your children's psychological and social needs are very important and can best be met by your maintaining an active role in their lives.

Many men fortunately have custody arrangements which allow them personally to see that these needs are met. They are able to grow and develop alongside their children. An active parent discovers a reciprocal relationship. While his impact on children is strong and beneficial, so too is the impact their children have on them. Children's many contributions influence fathers' lives, making them more complete and rewarding. In helping meet their children's basic needs, fathers often find their basic needs met, too.

Fathers with different custody arrangements must rely upon the children's mother to meet these needs. Fathers who conscientiously care about their children's welfare will try to strike a relationship with the children's mother which permits and encourages her to insure their children's basic needs are being met.

Understanding Children's Growth and Development

Recall for a minute the birth of your first child, your initial thoughts and feelings toward your child, your child's homecoming, your first few days and nights with this infant, its first words and steps. You have witnessed many significant events and have informally acquired much knowledge about your children and others.

Your children and others do not remain static. Their bodies, minds, and other qualities change continuously. Thus, in order to be knowledgeable about children, you need to have some appreciation for the major changes which occur from birth through adolescence.

Some of the major milestones marking important developmental signs are discussed below. Knowledge of child development allows you to understand the past, to take better care of the present, and to anticipate the future. Fathers play an important role during all phases of a child's development. Once the child is delivered, mothers have no natural superiority in the raising and caring of children. Fathers routinely assume the most important child-rearing tasks in other cultures. You can choose to do this, too.

Years 0 to 2. Birth may be man's most traumatic moment. He immediately passes from a state of balance and comfort in which all needs are met on demand to one of imbalance and discomfort in which his needs are not always met. His five senses suddenly become alive. Muscular and neurological development proceed from his head to his feet and from the midpoint of his body outwardly. Thus, the head and neck muscles develop first, while those in his toes develop last. The bones, like a newly laid egg, now are soft and gradually harden until adolescence. Many infants will sit up at 6 months, crawl and stand with help at 9 months, walk with support at 12 months, stand alone at 14 months, and walk without support at 16 months. Though some infants are born with teeth, most acquire the first half dozen by their first birthday, thus permitting them to eat non-soft foods. During this first year or two, a child's growth is more rapid than at any time in his life. Between birth and 2, he may double his original height (of about 20 inches) and triple his original weight (of about 7 pounds).

Fathers need to feed, fondle, and talk to their babies. The babies need a father's love, praise, and attention. They also need protection. Punishment, particularly physical punishment, must not be used. Provide a variety of sights and sounds to this neophyte. Above all, your infant needs to learn to trust you as a warm and caring father.

The Terrible Two's. You witness a change from an infant who is dependent and only responsive to stimuli to a young child who quickly is gaining a sense of independence (through his increased mobility) and is becoming a producer of stimuli. Language development is his most dramatic accomplishment. However, his physical development is occurring too. Though initially top heavy (a big head and long arms), growth now is concentrated in his legs, hands, and feet. He is gaining greater control over his involuntary muscles, and his nervous system is becoming more complex and refined.

Fathers have much to provide during this year. Rules are being consistently established and reinforced through praise and discipline to help children learn what is expected of them. A child's desire to become more independent requires fathers to assume more supervisory responsibilities. We have heard the stories of the inquisitive 2-year-old drowning after stumbling across the yard and into a neighbor's backyard pool. Cause-and-effect relationships are being explored and require an understanding parent who patiently and repeatedly explains things to the inquisitive mind. And don't forget toilet training. This occurs about now, too.

The Preschool Years: 3 to 5.   During this period, a child's days are characterized by four activities: running, talking, eating, and sleeping. Muscle and bone development continues but at a rate slower than that seen during the first three years. The child's climbing, running, jumping, pulling, pushing, hoping, and balancing promote larger muscle development. As these words imply, these are active years. Children are acquiring greater endurance, a slower heart rate, and higher blood pressure. Language and intellectual development occur jointly and advance rapidly. The brain has 75% of its final weight by 2 and 90% by 6. The child's receptive understanding of language allows him to understand others and to go beyond his immediate environment through television, radio, and telephone. His expressive language allows him to articulate his needs and ideas, to interact with others, and to begin socializing.

Children begin to form strong relationships with their fathers. Your being available to them enables them to become more self-confident and to learn to do activities in adult-like ways. Their incessant question asking may get on your nerves, yet try to answer them completely and by relating new information to something they know already. Promote logical problem-solving skills. Finally, don't be disturbed if your children masturbate. All children do. It's not dirty or evil and won't make them go blind. Ask them to do it in their room and not in public. Masturbating in public soon decreases.

The Elementary School Years: 6 to 12.   Primary emphasis now shifts from physical and muscular development (though they remain important) to academic, cognitive, and social development. Basic reading and math skills are acquired (in grades one through three) and later applied and refined (in grades four and above). Cognitive development flourishes through improved judgment, reasoning, and concept formation. Cooperative games and sports become popular, and parents become spectators at their children's soccer, baseball, and football games. Music lessons, scouting, and various hobbies begin, too. Social maturation is apparent. Boys and girls joyfully play together and intense but ever-changing friendships develop.

Around 12, first girls and then boys cautiously venture out to establish special friends of the opposite gender.

When your children are 12, be prepared for orthodontist bills, too. Most permanent teeth are in, and braces and retainers may be needed. The body is filling out, the limbs are lengthening, the bones are harder (and more easily broken), muscle tissue has increased and added strength, fine motor cordination advances quickly, food consumption increases, and the need for prolonged sleep decreases.

Many men see these years as the golden period of fatherhood. Strong relationships with both daughters and sons emerge, fathers actively teach them basic living skills and moral values, and mutual respect and love are exchanged. The absence of strong and consistent father-child relationships at this time can be detrimental to both fathers and children.

Help and encouragement with regular school work and special projects are expected. Attendance at PTA meetings, scouts, and concerts can be energizing to you and them. Teaching them how to kick balls, bait hooks, tie shoe skates, or various other sports provides lifelong benefits to them and lifelong memories to you. Participate with them. Everyone benefits.

Children also need to be informed about physical and sexual changes they soon will experience. Discussions about the physical and emotional characteristics of puberty can help them approach this next stage with confidence. Discussions about reproduction and sex can begin during the preschool years and increase in sophistication as the children mature. Later, the importance of sensitivity toward the emotional and tender aspects of love-making should be discussed.

Children will search various sources for answers and ideas to their many questions. Your presence and willingness to communicate provide invaluable resources to them. Don't assume your importance is proportionate to the amount of time your children spend at home or with you. Some fathers feel their children consider their home a place to eat, sleep, change clothes, and get money. Your children are counting on your being available when they need you.

Don't give up on your children. Maintain confidence in them through their darkest hours, praying that they have the abilities to resolve the majority of their questions and problems and the knowledge to seek wise advice on those matters of greatest importance. Stand by to help, not to interfere. They need to experience both the joy of success and the agony of defeat.

Children's basic values also stabilize and mature during these years. They look to their parents as possible models for them. Their perceptions of how you handled yourself and your relationships with their mother and them following the divorce will have a major impact on their values and on the strategies they use in overcoming their own problems. Children who observe their parents face crises by withdrawing or expressing hostility and blame are likely to use similar strategies. Those who see their parents use more effective problem-solving techniques are better able to resolve their crises.

Stick by your values and maintain rules. Find a blend which allows your children the freedom to explore within areas of relative safety while identifying boundaries which should not be exceeded.

The Stormy Teens: 13 to 18. Inconsistency may best describe this period. Increased but irregular hormonal development stimulates the development of sex glands which produces sex hormones. This triggers menarche (with girls often having their first period between 11 and 15) and erections (boys' sexual development tends to lag 1 to 2 years behind girls'). Children become preoccupied with their bodies, hair, and clothes. How they feel about their body is more important than an evaluation of their body based on objective criteria. The self-image of boys is hurt by being small and having underdeveloped muscles and facial defects. The self-image of girls is hurt by being tall, stocky, flat chested, and having facial defects; the ideal is a small, delicately built figure and no facial blemishes. Failure to develop normal body features may result in social rejection, feelings of sexual and social inadequacies, and a poor self-concept. Late maturers tend to be more anxious and attention seeking, less popular, and followers rather than leaders.

Academic and cognitive development somehow gets squeezed in between one's first love, telephone calls, movies, pizzas, parties, and part-time jobs. Academic specialization begins in grades eight or nine and continues throughout high school. Many students need help in selecting courses, in deciding on their program of work (that is, whether to pursue a college-bound, vocational, or business program), in developing and displaying good study skills, and in maintaining their motivation through the bad as well as the good teachers.

Questions about dating, after-school jobs, cars (and motorcycles for boys), and house chores dot conversations almost daily. "Senioritis," a social-emotional malaise, afflicts all 12th graders. Its symptoms include increased social activity, less interest in school work, and worry and concern about what follows high school. Marriage for some is strongly considered.

Recall the image of children's development resembling a rock rolling down a mountain. At middle to late adolescence the direction and velocity characterizing development are well established. Your influence at this time, though still important, is less than it was in earlier years. Your influence is strengthened by the examples you set and the encouragement you provide. Your children need your love, support, and reassurance. Through these they develop confidence in themselves, in others, and toward their future. Talking with them about daily events in their lives and yours encourages an interchange which allows you both to understand one another more completely and realistically. Make sure adult topics such as family and career planning, spending and saving money, selecting and maintaining friendships, courtship, love-making, and other important issues are integrated into your conversations. Recognize, too, that you may be presenting a man's viewpoint. Your children need to know your views and those of others. Thus, encourage your children to seek answers from other trustworthy sources. Anticipate that inconsistencies in your children's behaviors and attitudes may occur and that you should not overreact to small or temporary changes. Encourage your children to accept responsibility for their welfare at home and elsewhere (for example, to do well at school and to find part-time employment), and to take an interest in community, state, national, and international events. Fathering is an exciting privilege. It also carries many responsibilities. Children's development should not be left to chance factors. Active guidance by father will help insure healthy, happy children.

Your children, no matter what their ages, are likely to develop healthy and happy lives when you and other important persons act in the following ways:

- love then abundantly and openly
- show love toward others
- discipline them constructively
- spend time together
- teach solid values by word and action
- display mutual respect
- listen to promote understanding and communication
- offer help and guidance
- foster independence
- establish realistic expectations

By demonstrating these 10 characteristics to your children, you encourage the development of healthy persons who can better withstand various forms of disappointment and stress, particularly those which arise at this time of divorce.

4

Divorce:

Its General Effects on Children

Thomas Oakland

"And how are your children doing?" How many times have you been asked that question? Your friends and family may assume that you or your former wife wanted to separate in order to seek a better life. But the children are different. They often are viewed as the victims—the vulnerable ones caught up in the middle of a controversy involving two self-centered adults.

Fathers have hundreds of questions about the effects of divorce on their children. "What is likely to happen to my children during and following a divorce? What troubles, if any, are they likely to experience? Will a teenager react differently than a preschooler? Are daughters more affected than sons? Will it always be this way? How can I help?" There is much that fathers can do. The ways you handle your divorce and relationships with your children significantly influence how they come through this period.

Fathers who divorce should not feel guilty about the emotional scars divorce leaves on children. Children's major problems are not caused by divorce. They occur when their basic needs are not recognized and met. At the time of the divorce, children's emotions usually are mixed. They feel anger and resentment toward their parents for having these problems which disrupt *their* lives. They may secretly or openly wish that their parents will get back together. Though they genuinely care about what is happening to their father and mother, their deeper concerns rest on what is happening to them.

Though they feel anger and resentment, they also may feel relief that the bickering, sulking, fighting, and malicious behaviors between their parents will end.

Major problems also arise when the stress associated with divorce is added to other already stressful situations. Children often cope very well with divorce when other parts of their lives are going well. However, the problems associated with a divorce may overload an already overtaxed system, causing a severe breakdown in some children.

Each family member responds to divorce differently. Some children seem more vulnerable and susceptible to family difficulties. They may become angry, even hostile, toward their parents and siblings in response to the disintegration they see about them. Sons, more than daughters, follow this pattern. Daughters, on the other hand, may direct their anger inwardly. They may accept responsibility for their parents separating and valiantly try to reunite them. When all else fails, they may form a strong emotional dependence on either their father or mother. Some children seem more removed from the effects of divorce. They may find stability through their school work, after-school activities, friends, and extended family. In general, divorce seems to be hardest on younger children, sons, temperamental children, those with a history of psychological or social problems, and those who are less adaptable and need a consistent environment. Fathers of children with these characteristics should be particularly aware of their adjustment and development and should consider getting professional help for them if needed.

Though each child responds to divorce differently, most children seem to go through similar developmental patterns. Good judgment shown by fathers during these stages helps to promote a healthy family and children.

Children's Passages Through Divorce

No two people experience and respond to divorce in the same way. Children's reactions to divorce depend on a variety of factors: the stage of the divorce, their ages and gender, the stability within their environment, and quality and quantity of contacts with parents, particularly their father. Each of these areas is explored below.

Normal Family Life

The setting typically starts with one or more children in a family which is fairly stable and meets the children's basic needs. The children love both their mother and father though they may be closer emotionally to one. They sense and accept as natural the equilibrium and organization within their home.

Stage One: A Prelude

The first stage is marked by some disquieting signs that the stability is cracking. Various changes are noticeable. One or both parents may be away more from the house, more upset, and less tolerant. Meals have changed, too. The family eats together irregularly, meals go unprepared, and less care is given to preparing favorite foods. Dad and Mom argue more, often over trivial matters. They stay mad longer and don't joke or kiss one another. In fact, the increase in interpersonal conflicts among the parents may also extend to an increase in interpersonal conflicts among the siblings. Home becomes a less happy, loving place. Traditional patterns seem to be changing. The family's stability and equilibrium are being destroyed.

Stage Two: Discovery

The second stage is one that is remembered forever, although it's usually the shortest: the children are informed that their parents are separating and probably divorcing. This tends to be one of life's most intense and emotional moments. A confluence of feelings and emotions may surge through each family member: sadness, hurt, rejection, love, denial, relief, despair, hope, aloneness, togetherness. We will return to this second stage to discuss some helpful strategies for getting through it.

This predivorce period can produce severe stress and anxiety in children. Their intact family is dissolving. Some children feel responsible for the difficulties and attempt to reconcile their parents.

Children may demonstrate extreme behaviors in attempting to reunite Mom and Dad. They may run away one day and refuse to leave their room the next. Others may demonstrate extremes in their emotions. A little Miss Sunshine, trying to bring happiness to all, may suddenly cry and become sullen at not having the power to work things out between the parents. Many children become ill physically or emotionally, some through real and others through imagined causes. During this pre-divorced period be prepared for the possibility that the family changes your children are experiencing will produce various disruptions in their medical, social, and emotional behaviors.

Stage Three: Disorganization

The third stage is marked by personal and family disequilibrium and disorganization. It occurs when one parent—and perhaps the children—move from their home. For some, the move is within the neighborhood; for others, it is across town, across the state, or across the country. Many of the old habits are broken and a sense of disorganization prevails.

Children who move face the added difficulties of making new friends, adjusting to new schools, discovering recreational resources, and living in a strange house and neighborhood. Children fortunate enough to remain in their home still often receive less attention from their parents, are asked to do more for themselves, and may be treated quite inconsistently.

A single parent now is faced with more home and financial responsibilities while still trying to recover from the hurt, stress, and shock associated with the divorce. Because the family's resources have changed, less money is available for clothes, recreation, and miscellaneous items.

The first year tends to be the worst. Various family members—especially the parents—are likely to have more physical illnesses, many of which are psychosomatic, caused by a depressed emotional state. Psychosomatic illnesses do not respond well to typical medical treatments and thus linger. A debilitating cycle may be created: The illnesses sap their weight, persistence, and energy. Self-doubts and worries increase as do erratic behaviors as they frantically search for solutions to overwhelming problems. Problems at work may intensify. Attention to basic physical and psychological needs together with sound problem-solving strategies will help avert this cycle.

First-year adjustment problems often are most acute in women and sons. Women may be overwhelmed by stress and anxiety. They may be inconsistent and less able to make decisions about themselves and the children. Men should be prepared to experience the repercussions of these conditions through their interaction with their former wives and their children. Children, particularly boys remaining in the custody of their mothers, also tend to experience great stress associated with their loss of a parent, conflicts in allegiances, household changes, and vague uncertainties. Expressions of anger, depression, fears, and guilt are common.

The first year of the divorce can be tumultuous. Conflicts and problems increase. Because the children likely are living in a single-parent family for the first time, they have more responsibilities and less parental attention. Some children effectively experience the loss of both parents if one remains away and the other works 8 hours or more each day. Also parents frequently are preoccupied with their own problems and needs, often flirt with new lifestyles, and are not aware of the depth of their children's problems.

Any move takes children from the familiar to the unfamiliar and adds to their sense of loss, conflict, and uncertainty as well. The greater the instability, the more difficult their transition, and the more likely they will show stronger emotions such as anger, fear, and depression. Even older children may temporarily behave like 3-and 4-year-olds by wanting to sleep with the remaining parent, bed wetting, refusing to go to school or exhibiting other signs of anxiety and dependency.

While dark winterlike clouds hide many rays of hope during the first year, the second year following the divorce can be characterized differently—and more positively. Stability and order begin to return to children's lives. Their parents' lives also tend to be more regular. Out of the unknown emerge new family forms in which the roles of each person are being defined. Whereas, during the first year, crisis appeared to follow crisis, during the second year crises are becoming resolved. Hurts fade into acceptance, fears dissolve into confidence, and anger is used more constructively to seek solutions to problems.

Adjustments occur through productive habits and consistent life styles. Family members seem to gain a sense of control over their lives again.

Fathers will have found ways to balance work, home, and social activities. While they may have missed some work during and shortly after the divorce, they now are able to be at work regularly. In fact, some men find a renewed sense of stimulation and dedication to their jobs after the weight of the divorce is removed.

Men learn, too, that food gets purchased, meals cooked, clothes cleaned, and dishes washed. Domestic responsibilities take time but with proper time management fit into daily schdules. New relationships with their children emerge and become somewhat habitual. Child care and after-school activities for the children seem to be going smoothly. If the children are seen less often, many fathers strive for more meaningful relationships with each child. They may feel great pain in being deprived of a more active role in raising children. Seeing the children only every other weekend places severe strains on their relationships. A strong tendency exists to plan super times—the latest movies, ballgames, parties, trips out of town, restaurant meals—because of a desire to show their children a good time and that they love them. Fathers want their children to like them. Many fathers soon find, however, that these honeymoon weekends have an opposite effect. They do not allow fathers and children to develop personalized ways of relating to each other.

Resignation is one way to cope with problems. Fathers often want to do more, to have stronger influence. However, by the end of the second year, they likely accept their fate and hope for the best. Unfortunately, many fathers withdraw from their children. For them the pain of irregular and incomplete fathering is too much to bear.

Mothers' initial fears and anxieties about making it alone are lessened. The initial stress of relocating is over. The children are more settled and household routines estblished. A new part-time or full-time job, though not totally fulfulling professionally, gives them a renewed sense of confidence and needed money. This job may be temporary as they consider others which offer more challenge, opportunities, and rewards.

Increased confidence also emerges as women begin dating again. The experience is strange. They learn to cope with sexual innuendos and advances. They feel good about themselves as their social groups expand to include people who are supportive and interested in them.

Children may show widely different adjustment patterns during this second year. Adjustment differences appear because of differences in their age, gender, and temperament (more about this later). Perhaps the most important factor influencing their adjustment is the extent to which their basic needs are met.

Preschool children often have little self-control. During disruptions like those which occur in divorce, young children tend to exhibit more anxiety and even less self-control. Lacking self-discipline and control, they look for structure from their parents and other adults. Family relationships become the most important quality influencing their development.

Their adjustment during this second year is good if they were nurtured and cared for in a consistent fashion during the last 12 to 18 months. Home and preschool routines must be organized and regular. Big doses of physical attention should be provided regularly. Differences in children's emotional and social needs can be met by allotting some individual time with each child. Avoid day-care centers in which each teacher has many children. Strive for a home in which a warm, loving adult provides quality care to five or fewer well-adjusted youngsters. In general, avoid profit-hungry commercial day-care programs whose programs tend to be highly structured and follow the book while teacher turnover rates and teacher-pupil ratios are high.

Elementary-age children often are asked to grow up quickly and to assume many home responsibilities. Parents also may rely upon them for emotional support. With increased demands, children often feel overwhelmed. They also may be told, or decide for themselves, that they are ineffective in meeting their parents' requests for help. Unsolved problems lead to feelings of incompetence. Resentment often follows.

This pattern too frequently occurs for boys in families with mothers as the single parent. A message is communicated that David now is the "man of the house" with added duties and responsibilities. Though he enjoys his new status, he resents the duties—and resents not having his dad around too. His frustrations and anger are directed toward his mother. While mother-son relationships during the first year seem acceptable, they may unravel during the second year. The impact of divorce tends to be stronger and more immediate, pervasive, and enduring on sons than on daughters. They are more apt to show their problems by being noncompliant and aggressive and having interpersonal problems with teachers and peers.

For elementary-age girls, the picture is somewhat different. During the second year their loneliness and anxieties often fade. They seem to accept their fate and at this time do not exhibit the same rebellious and aggressive conduct as their brothers. Though their major problems seem to have subsided, they may reappear during adolescence. When elementary-age girls enter adolescence they may be rebellious toward their mothers and want to move away from home, preferably to move in with their fathers.

Adolescents may experience fewer post-divorce problems than younger children. While the self-worth of younger children is often judged by how they are treated at home, the self-worth of adolescents is more broadly based and includes strong reliance in peer acceptance. Thus, adolescents are less dependent on the family as the single and sole source of support.

The initial pain and anger experienced in the first few months dissipate considerably by the second year. Teenagers are better able to assign responsibilities for the divorce, to resolve conflicts in loyalties, and to successfully cope with domestic demands.

Regaining a Normal Life

The third and last stage, often occurring during the third to fourth years, finds the individuals and family more consolidated, reorganized, equilibrated, and exhibiting healthy living patterns. No, there are no story-book endings, nor do all families and individuals reach this stage. Family problems continue, often at a rate and with a severity higher than those in a nuclear family. Problems between mother and sons seem most persistent, particular when the father does not have regular and frequent contacts with his children. Relationships probably are weak if continuous contact was not maintained. Fathers who moved to a different city or state will be most separate from their children.

About one child in three remains very unhappy and dissatisfied with life. Loneliness and depression linger when the custodial parent is not home after school and is heavily involved socially on weekends.

Most people come to realize that divorce is a major milestone, neither to be denied nor dwelled upon. Order and regularity return and the major functions continue: home, work, play, education, social relationships.

Men likely will remarry and may have more children; contacts with their former wives are minimal and largely involve the children. Women seem less inclined to remarry. Relationships between children and their fathers are likely to be strong if continuous contacts were maintained with them during the last few years. In fact, one or more children may have decided to leave their mother and move in with dad.

A remarriage probably provides greater happiness and stability to men's lives but causes children to experience many changes again. Children must reenter a two-parent family, adjust to a new parent, probably more siblings, and even a different house and school. The stresses and dislocations children encountered before may reappear. Their adjustment is helped if the children feel accepted, if the new family members share the children's values, and if they work cooperatively. A remarriage will work only when all partners invest the energy and commitment to make it happen.

Remarriage may be particularly threatening to girls who may fantasize about taking care of dad. Stepmothers and stepdaughters face the greatest problems. An important place must be found for the children and assurances provided to them. The new wife's attitudes and behaviors can do much to foster feelings that they are genuinely wanted and needed. Recognize, too, the father's important responsibilities in helping to integrate his children and those of his new wife into a new family structure.

In Summary

Divorce is not a single event, but stimulates a confluence of experiences likely to produce social, emotional, financial, and educational changes in all persons. Each family member will respond to divorce differently. As a father, you need to anticipate what may occur, to understand what your chlildren are experiencing, to minimize their hardships, and to help them whenever possible to make a healthy transition.

For children, divorce usually means the break-up of a stable and organized family and home and a transition to one which at first is less stable and disorganized. In searching for stability and organization, children will look to adults for direction. They will also experiment with different roles. The ways in which your children respond to divorce will vary widely. Yet, they likely will go through similar developmental patterns. They will experience both success and failure. The quest hopefully will result in their finding a reorganized life which provides renewed stability and a new equilibrium.

FACTORS INFLUENCING CHILDREN'S ADJUSTMENT

The effects of divorce on children can be viewed from many dimensions. The effects of age and time on adjustment have just been considered, but factors other than age and time also have a decided impact on children's development. Though prior discussions have emphasized some, at least five need re-emphasis here because of their importance: economic changes, mother-father conflicts, continued contacts with both parents, gender, and age factors.

Economic Changes

Economic changes, usually hardships, follow divorce. The custodial parent likely is working full time, thus providing fewer contact hours between parent and children. Erratic meal and bed times and less attention to children's school work often follow. Legal expenses can take half or more of your yearly net income. With less income and more expenses, some families find it necessary to cut back on big budget items: home, food, transportation, and clothing. Children may need to adjust to a lower standard of living in a smaller, more spartanly furnished home in a poorer neighborhood. They may resent not being able to buy as many new clothes or have as much money to spend freely.

Some will get part-time jobs to supplement their income. Unless closely scrutinized, they may spend less and less time at home. Adolescents who are particularly inclined toward rejecting parental authority find power in their new economic freedom and try to sidestep parental authority.

Continued Conflicts between Mother and Father

Divorce signals the end to your legally sanctioned union but does not signal the end to all relationships with your former wife. Divorce for most men involves gradual stages of separation and disentanglement. Marital discord, hatred, deception, and jealousies that existed during the marriage may not fade easily following the divorce. Actions of one parent during and following the divorce may serve to intensify acrimonious feelings of the other. Given these conditions, one or both parents may use the children in psychological and social warfare toward the other. The battle is staged by first openly criticizing one parent in front of the children. This is followed by broader salvos which enumerate all past flaws and blemishes. Of course, comments by a parent pointing out similarities between a child and bad characteristics of the other parent ("You are just like your father!") can have devastating effect on the child.

The attempt by one parent to demean the other is a perverse way to vent anger and frustrations and to get revenge by dividing the children's loyalties. Battles may continue to be fought over alimony, child support, visitation, or numerous other issues.

Children's adjustment to divorce is made more difficult when mother-father conflicts are highly intense and carried out over a longer time period. Children want to be loyal to and receive support from both parents. Instead of finding strength and help from their parents, children often encounter new problems. Problems can become most acute for children who identify strongly with and love the parent being maligned. Continued exposure to a mother's criticisms of father may severely hamper the sex-role development of girls and may be especially traumatic to boys. Some children form a general impression that adults are not able to solve problems actively in an equitable and moral way.

Continued Contact with Both Parents

Children's adjustment is best when they have regular and frequent contacts with nurturing parents. The importance of the father's role as a noncustodial parent during and following the divorce is well understood. Fathers who have frequent and direct contacts and involvement with children have a greater influence on children. The adjustment of both the children and fathers is quicker and more healthy, and problems between mothers and children are lessened.

Fathers' indirect influence on their children also is important. By providing regular child support money, fathers help to insure their children's basic needs for food, clothing and shelter are met. Fathers' continued financial help fosters children's feeling of confidence that their parents care for them now and will continue to do so in the future.

Similar generalizations seem to hold true when fathers have primary custody. In this situation regular and frequent mother-child contacts further their adjustment and thus the father's, too.

Gender Differences

Fathers who are fortunate to have both sons and daughers often recognize some differences in how they respond to the divorce. Compared to the impact on girls, the impact of divorce on boys tends to be harder, affects more areas of their lives, and is longer lasting.

Boys more frequently revert back to infantile behaviors and become grossly dependent and apathetic. They are more willing to become aggressive and noncompliant; disobeying their mothers becomes a frequent occurrence. Problems with neighborhood and school friends may be common. Teachers also may report aggression, behavior disorders, and academic negligence. With boys, problem behaviors also may be more persistent, lasting three or more years.

Whereas boys externalize their anger and frustration through acting them out, girls internalize their anger and frustration. They tend to become passive and dependent. Crying and withdrawing also may be common. Older girls may become particularly solicitous toward their fathers, hoping to find some amicable solution to their relationship.

Age Differences

Children's passages through divorce, as we have seen, are influenced by the stage of the divorce, changes in income and standards of living, mother-father conflicts, degree of contact with both parents, and the child's gender.

Another factor, the child's age, is perhaps the most important. A 2-year-old will respond to divorce very differently than a 12-year-old. By examining their developmental characteristics in light of situations they encounter in a divorce, you can understand your children better and help them minimize the difficulties of divorce.

Children differ in many characteristics. Though height and weight may be the most obvious, they are the least important. More important are differences in mental, social, and emotional qualities.

Infants and preschool children have the fewest developed qualities. Their needs are met largely by caring adults who see that their basic medical, biological, safety, psychological, and social needs are met. Their self-control is low, and their dependency is high.

While they initially expect to see both parents daily, their lives are not significantly disrupted by a divorce so long as one nurturing adult continues to provide the needed protection, food, warmth, love, and stimulation.

The infant's and preschooler's adjustment to divorce is enhanced by a well-organized home in which basic needs are provided. Times for meals, naps, playing, toileting, bedtime, and other daily events should occur regularly and consistently. Infants and preschoolers must be able to trust and depend upon their world.

Parental authority is strongest during these years and lessens as children grow into adults. They need to be guided by adults demonstrating mature judgments.

During these years the world of young children is restricted to their home (and day-care setting) and family. Thus, the quality of the home more strongly influences preschool children than those at older ages who can seek food, shelter, and love elsewhere. The needs of youngsters are met only by their home. Thus, an organized home providing consistent and quality care by mature persons in an atmosphere of love and concern for their basic needs will help infants and preschoolers through a divorce.

Children between 6 and 12 are distinctly different. Their mental and social abilities are more mature, they have greater mobility, more friends, a broader range of emotions, and a greater command of language. School occupies most of their day, while organized sports or music, playing with neighborhood friends, or TV consume late afternoon and evening hours. They, too, have the same basic needs as preschoolers. The difference lies in their ability to provide for many of their needs.

School-age children remain highly dependent on the family for support and sustenance. Moreover, they now realize their dependency and seek an environment which provides answers to questions and help in identifying and overcoming problems. To them, home should be a source of support, not a source of trouble or turmoil.

Divorce brings changes and upheavals to the family. Children may not understand the full meaning of a divorce and become confused. Their confusion is compounded when the parents act secretly and do not inform children of what is happening, why the divorce is occurring, and what their immediate future holds for them.

In an attempt to add order to their lives, children often distort their parents' motives, behaviors, and feelings. Some children will blame themselves for the breakup. Others work valiantly for their reconciliation. They may have strong feelings as to what should be done and yet no power to control what will be done. Their frustration can be overwhelming.

The custodial parent may look upon the children for more and more emotional support. This parent also may ask the children to make long strides toward self-sufficiency about the home by taking on various household tasks—shopping, cleaning, laundry, cooking, and home repairs. When the parent expresses dissatisfaction with the speed or quality of the child's action, disappointment and confusion well into sadness. Crying, withdrawal, or anger often follow.

School-age children need information from both parents as to what is happening, why it is occurring, and what the outcomes may be. They want to know how the divorce affects them. They are less concerned about how the divorce affects their parents.

Take time to talk with your children regularly and to elicit their views and comments. They need to know they can have no major effect on the divorce but may have a role in deciding their futures. Retain as much stability and consistency as possible within the family, school, and other areas of their lives. This promotes greater confidence and insures continued independence.

Adolescence is a period of rapid physical growth, sexual development, and broadening social activities outside the home. They are less dependent on the family as the single and sole source of information and support. Some adults are deceived into believing that, by looking beyond the home, adolescents are less affected by events in the home. Adolescents look to their home for support and stability and to their parents as potential models for themselves and their mates.

Prior to the separation and divorce, their family has been intact for 12 or more years. The impressions formed of their home and family come from diverse experiences through the years, including less-than-perfect parents and various home crises.

Adolescents often experience considerable pain and anger when their parents first divorce. The divorce adds to the turmoil and stress they already experience due to their physical and social changes. A home traditionally is characterized as a place of love and support, and parents are characterized as being suitable models for their children. Both home and parents now may be viewed more as caricatures than realities. The children are often disappointed in their parents' inability to work things out.

Some adolescents revert back to earlier stages and behave like children, even preschoolers. Delinquent behaviors including stealing, lying, and drug or alcohol abuse may surface. Loss of appetite and sleep may appear.

Intense feelings of loyalty may be displayed toward one parent. Frequently, sons side with mothers, and daughters side with fathers. Their loyalty and other intense feelings may cloud their judgments and cause them to distort information. Adolescents who were somewhat alienated from one or both parents before the divorce draw even further away following the divorce.

Adolescents also are more knowledgeable and intelligent than younger children. They may have anticipated the divorce and were aware of marital discord. Thus, after the initial shock and impact, they are more able to rebound and to lead a normal life. They have greater resources to cope with domestic, financial, and social changes. They are more in control of their lives.

Compared to younger children, adolescents seem better able to compartmentalize their problems. Their problems at home may not disrupt their on-going educational and vocational obligations or peer relationships.

Thus, be prepared to help your adolescents through their initial pain and anger. This requires patience, persistence, and communication. They feel they have a right to be heard and to be informed. While encouraging them to talk with mature friends and other adults, make sure you take time to discuss your thoughts and feelings with them. They need information and assurance. Avoid the temptation to solicit their support or to unleash an attack on their mother.

In Summary

The time you and your children spend together is a vital factor. The amount of time and how it is used strongly influence their development and yours. As a rule, the more time you spend together, the better. Many fathers find they have more time to be with their children during the separation and following the divorce than before. During this period, continue as many prior obligations and habits as possible. Take them to athletic practice and games, scouts, and shopping. Help with homework. Attend church together. Continue with important routines which have been established. Find a happy balance between doing nothing (some children rightly complain that TV watching comprises too of their time) and having each minute committed. Be together in ways which each enjoys. Combine new activities with maintaining pleasant traditions. Provide time for talking and listening, loving and caring. Children love and appreciate dads for what they personally bring to relationships. Spending your money on them, though appreciated, is less important than spending your time with them. This allows you to maintain and further relationships so important to living a healthy, balanced life.

Some people will tell you that the *quality* of time, not its *quantity*, is the important component to happiness. That notion is incorrect. Both are important. Realize that you cannot have quality time with your children unless you have sufficiently long periods of time together. Quality relationships between children and their day-a-week father are difficult to achieve. Competing responsibilities that day, scheduling the day's events tightly, tension springing from the need to maximize each minute, and avoiding certain topics for fear of offending each other—these and other factors prevent a father and children from establishing a normal and relaxed relationship.

PREPARING CHILDREN FOR THE DIVORCE

Telling children your marriage is over may be the most difficult task you ever face. Even if the news is not a complete surprise, you know they will feel hurt, confused, rejected, frustrated, lonely, and so many other qualities you do not want your children to experience, especially at your doing!

Your feelings—similar to those of the children plus others—may burst forth too. You also may feel a strong sense of defeat at not having succeeded at maintaining a marriage and family. In the eyes of many, divorce is a distinct sign of failure. Telling your children about the divorce may be telling them you have failed yourself and them. This is very difficult, particularly if you have been bred on the importance of achievement and success.

The children will find out about the divorce. The question is, who tells them, and how is it done? Some children come home from school to discover one parent has moved out. Their surprise may turn into a state of shock, not knowing why their parent left, or if he or she ever will return. Other children are informed through the children of family friends or neighbors in whom their mother or father have confided. In these examples and countless others, they are told by persons who have no right to know this vital information before your children do.

Your children need to be informed about the divorce by you. Their mother should be there, too. This helps to insure that they know you care about them enough to go through this agony *with them*, that they get the facts correctly, and that your talking with them helps establish a relationship in which you can continue to discuss various matters associated with the divorce.

If you tell the children, you control the accuracy of the information they receive and initially need. The children always need the truth though they do not need to know all the details at once. They also need to know you and their mother care deeply about them. Only you can convey this through your presence, your words, and your feelings.

Tell the children when there are no distractions, and you have sufficient time to talk at length. Springing it on the children in the morning before school or following a heated argument with your wife must be avoided. You all need time to understand and discuss many issues, and to listen sympathetically to each other. Both parents should plan ahead to anticipate the questions their children will raise. After learning that the divorce is to occur, they need various forms of assurance. They must know that they are not the cause of the divorce, that their parents both still love them, and that plans have been made which insure their continued welfare. This includes plans for housing, schooling, and continued time with their parents and other family members.

Questions about why you are divorcing at first can be answered by general comments, such as: "You probably know your mother and I have not been happy for a long time. Your mother and I no longer love each other. We find that we have grown apart, that we are very different people, and that we are not happy living together." Explanations which place the blame on one party, allude to sordid affairs, or emphasize the personal weaknesses of one spouse should be avoided. More exacting information, if necessary, may be discussed over time. At this beginning, try to communicate the basic information in a tone which includes assurance.

Of course, the amount of information you convey and how it is presented depends on the ages of your children. Many fathers have found it beneficial to gather all the children together and to inform them at the same time. This allows you to hold hands and provide other kinds of physical contact, to offer various forms of emotional support, to cry together, or just to be together during this important time. Crying should not be discouraged. Through crying, you share the pain and anxiety of separating and draw closer together. Being together as a family at this time can provide a strong symbol of support and assurance. Other parents may choose to discuss the divorce individually with their children, thus allowing them to consider the individual differences and needs of each child.

Your Continuing Relationships During the Separation. This initial discussion about the divorce is the first of hopefully many. You will have to talk about more specific details of the separation: when it will occur, custodial and other living arrangements, the division of property, and major changes (such as jobs or moving away). These talks should allow your children to express their concerns, to identify their preferences, and to offer suggestions. While you will not be able to accept all their suggestions, you will find that their solutions to some problems have merit. Moreover, their adjustment to the divorce and new living arrangements is furthered by knowing they can play a part in resolving problems.

Anticipate the possibility that some children, at first, will try to totally deny that the divorce is going to occur. This is a natural reaction which allows them to put unfavorable thoughts out of their mind. One young son, upon being told about the divorce, did not realize the consequences of the message, asked for a drink of water, and walked off. Many children will not be able or willing to accept the impact of what is said. They see their family intact right now. Continued discussions and moderate changes in the family will encourage a more realistic outlook. Also anticipate that, once children realize the reality, denial may turn to anger. The anger may be directed toward them or toward others (particularly, the custodial parent). The various ways children's feelings may come out are discussed in the next section. Techniques for dealing with them are also discussed.

5

Anticipating Children's Problems and Providing Help

Thomas Oakland

Three of the six most stressful events which involve children are associated with divorce. The divorce itself, separation, and remarriage hit as strongly as do a death of a parent, the child's becoming physically deformed, and the death of a brother or sister. Any one of these may trigger significant psychological and social problems which need your attention and perhaps professional help.

Children's response to your separation and divorce, as we have seen, can differ greatly. How you and their mother treat the children, their ages and gender, and custodial arrangements are but a few factors which influence your children's adjustment.

As a concerned father, you will want to know how they are responding to and coping with changes affecting their lives. You are able to observe signs of stress they exhibit at home. However, you will want to be aware of how the divorce may be affecting their behaviors in school, with their friends, and in the neighborhood and community.

Children's Behavior at Home

Children's behavior around the home suddenly may change. They may show signs of stress through changes in various habits and routines including what they eat, when they sleep, and how they dress and care for themselves. Sibling competition and jealousies may increase as may lying and other forms of dishonesty. In some cases, outright aggression toward family members occurs. Other children may want to return to earlier, happier times. Other signs can include their fantasizing life by playing with dolls and stuffed animals, their reverting to baby talk and sucking their thumb, or their becoming highly dependent on you to make decisions for them.

Your children are experiencing divorce for the first time. Sure, they know of other families who have gone through a divorce and have seen its effects on friends. However, because of their immaturity and lack of knowledge, you may find them trying to cope with new demands in various ways.

Punish Parents. Chris' value system became shattered to the point where he abandoned many of his values. He felt hurt and rejected because his parents did not live up to his ideals. Chris got back at his parents by displaying rebellious and delinquent behaviors in an attempt to embarrass his parents and demonstrate to them how it feels to have loved ones debase his important values and standards.

Seek New Identities. Nancy rejected the past and withdrew from the present by trying to establish a new identity. She changed her name, altered her hair style and color, bought new (often outlandish) clothes, selected new friends, developed new hobbies and interests, espoused different values, suddenly changed her religious affiliation, and in other ways tried to create a new image to match her desire for a new personality. Nancy's attempt to seek a new identity followed an attempt by one of her parents to make a number of major lifestyle changes.

Deny Problems. Robert faced divorce by not admitting it was occurring. When asked by friends if his parents were divorcing, he denied this and constructed a seemingly plausible explanation for their separation. His sister, Susan, admitted to the divorce but found it impossible to discuss problems for fear this would shatter an already delicate relationship she had with her parents.

Show Anxieties and Fears. Michael became very dependent on his mother, refusing to leave her side. He often refused to go to school and feigned sickness. Michael was particularly troubled by being left alone when his mother went out. He was afraid of the dark, complained about nightmares involving monsters harming him, and insisted on sleeping with his mother.

Become Depressed. Dee was listless for months. She was unmotivated, expressionless, and lethargic; friends stopped calling after she repeatedly refused to see them. Her grades plummeted, and she took less and less care of her clothes and room. Sometimes she would even withdraw into her room for days, often crying and refusing to eat. Her father was concerned that she may even attempt suicide.

Fathers often are able to detect consistent patterns in their children's behaviors. Some children will exhibit *conduct* disorders which are highly disturbing to others. These include attention-seeking behaviors, disruptiveness, fighting, hyperactivity, swearing, uncooperativeness, and temper tantrums. Chris exemplifies a child with a conduct disorder.

Other children exhibit *personality* disorders which show signs of internal conflicts. They include anxiety, depression, hypersensitivity, low self-confidence, disinterestedness, withdrawal, and fears. Though these signs may not be directly disturbing to others, they strongly signal the need for help. Nancy, Robert, and Michael show signs of a personality disorder. Children showing strong and persistent conduct or personality disorders need professional attention.

You'll notice the appearance of many of these behaviors immediately. Other changes may be more subtle and require more sensitivity. For example, the changes some children are going through may be reflected only in the contents of books, TV, and films they now prefer. Other children become confused in the face of ambiguities and insist that all doubts and uncertainties be removed. They honestly may be searching for a rigid differentiation between right and wrong and the boundaries which define what they can and cannot do.

Children's Behavior at School

Next to parents, teachers tend to know children best and have the greatest influence on them. If you have school-age children, develop a close dialgoue with their teachers. Inform them of the general home situation and alert them to possible problems (for example, psychosomatic illnesses or crying). They will be more understanding and supportive of the children. Also, ask them to inform you about your children's school behaviors. Be concerned about truancy, changes in grades or study habits, school conduct, and friendship patterns. During this time, some children will be lead by strong-willed peers in directions that are not healthy for them. The teachers may observe these and other important characteristics which you may not detect. Recognize, too, that their training in child development and their experiences with hundreds of children prepare them for this role. They are interested in your children's emotional and social development in addition to their academic development. Their help and advice may be valuable.

Children's Behavior in the Community. Neighbors, friends, church, school and club leaders also can become a form of silent partner helping you to be aware of what your children are doing and thinking while you are not around. Let them know your family is experiencing some changes. They can be helpful in informing you of gross misconduct. Their children may tell them events involving your children which you should be aware of. While you want to avoid a gestapo-like atmosphere, you want to maintain lines of communications which reach out to all segments of your children's life.

SIGNS OF STRESS IN CHILDREN

Everyone exhibits signs of stress during a divorce. For some children, these signs come and go and do not warrant great concern or professional attention. Professional attention is needed when children exhibit *many* stressful *signs* and when these behaviors *persist* over a longer period of time, are *displayed in various ways*, and become more *debilitating* to their normal routine. Consider the following signs of stress for each of your children. Check (✔) those you know occur some times. Put an asterisk (*) by those which have persisted for two months or more. Note too how generalized the behavior is. Be more concerned when your children display general signs of anxiety and stress in various situations. More generalized anxiety and stress also interefere with their normal daily routines.

Seek professional help for children if you check a number of behaviors, if you place an asterisk by three or more, if they show generalized signs which interfere with their normal daily routines.

A Checklist of Signs of Stress in Children

General Signs of Stress

Crying

Low tolerance for frustration

Changes in values or goals(ie, lying or stealing)

Absence of values or goals

Lacking of impulse control

Low self-confidence

Physically or verbally abusive toward self

Physically or verbally abusive toward others

Withdrawal from family or peers

Strong dependency on others

Denial of problems

Overwhelmed with ambiguities

Infantile-like behaviors (soiling, baby talk, plays with younger children)

Refusal to complete tasks

Lack of self-direction

Unable to discontinue activities known to be harmful to self or others

Signs of Stress at Home

Changes in established patterns (e.g. eating and sleeping)

Changes in self-care

Increased sibling competition and jealousy

Aggression toward family

Psychosomatic illnesses

Assuming the role as mother

Assuming the role as wife (excluding those of a sexual nature)

Changes in interests (TV programs, books, or movies)

Afraid of the dark

Not wanting to be left alone in a room

Awakening with nightmares

Refusing to leave home or the custodial parent

Signs of Stress in School

Truancy

Changes in friends

Avoids or rejects friends

Changes in grades

Changes in study habits

Discontinues club and group activities

Aggressive or withdrawal behavior

Easily frustrated

Signs of Stress With Friends

Changes in friendship patterns

Avoids good friends

Attracted toward peer of questionable character

Spends more time outside the home

Wants to move in with friends

Promiscuous sexual behaviors

Signs of Stress in the Neighborhood and Community

Exhibits delinquent behaviors

Stays out late for no apparently good reason

Leaves home without an expressed goal

Alcohol or drug abuse

Expresses a desire to be adopted by another family

Refuses to attend church, scouts, or other neighborhood or community social activities

These signs are signals that your chlidren need attention. Their stress signs may be their call for help.

The Family's Role

The American family is undergoing significant changes. Traditional roles and relationships between men, women, and children (and even grandparents, uncles, and aunts) are changing. Some people interpret this as a sign that the need for a family is changing. This probably is not correct.

The changes seen within families represent an attempt by its members to derive more benefits for themselves while remaining active as family members. The vast majority of people look to families to provide at least seven basic needs. Your effectiveness as a father can be judged by how well you contribute to forming a family which provides for these needs.

Security. All people seek protection from life-threatening events. The need to feel safe and secure is strong. The family and home are the major haven which provides this security. Substitutes for the family usually are not satisfactory.

Love. Everyone wants to receive and give love. This feeling of strong personal attachment and affection is more likely to occur within families which provide close, continuous contact. Reciprocal relationships often develop within families. Its members try to insure the welfare and happiness of each other.

Sense of Belonging. People need to feel they are a valuable member of a larger group, a family of people who share a loyalty to one another and a commitment to common goals. Persons who work by themselves and toward singular goals usually are lonely. Families tend to be the primary and most consistent group in which people affiliate and feel a sense of belonging.

Communication. Man is a communicating animal. An infant's ability to share and express its feelings and thoughts is first developed within the family. The family remains an important setting for developing communication skills. Difficulties in communicating often pose the biggest problems to a marriage. Thus, learning to .communicate effectively is one of the most important functions of families.

Need for change.   No person wants to remain totally static. We all have a natural tendency to change. If change occurs too slowly on its own, we actively seek change. Families provide ways to change in organized ways. For example, following adolescence, people need to develop intimate relationships. They later need to produce both offspring and work-related products as a sign of their maturity. Still later people need to experience integrity—a feeling that life has been worthwhile, that they have had their share of happiness, and that their lives have developed largely as they liked. Growth and change are always present and necessary. Families must be aware of the need for changes and provide for them.

Acceptance of Self and Others.   By providing security, love, affiliation, communication, and allowing for change, family members are able to come to know and accept themselves and others. Our society presently is struggling to live within its own resources. As people we also need to recognize and accept our assets and limitations and to learn to live with those features we cannot change. Families can effectively provide the setting in which the acceptance of self and others is learned.

Food, Clothing, and Shelter.   Families originally formed out of economic necessity. The social unit developed so as to help insure adequate supplies of food and clothing were available, and that the members of the unit were sheltered from physical dangers. These remain important needs of families. Their importance especially is seen at this time by the court in awarding child support and alimony payments to insure these needs are met.

Fathering

The stereotypical roles of mother and father in the traditional American family are characterized by a division of labor. Mothers have been described as the heart of the family, concerned with keeping the family together, raising children and maintaining a happy and loving home. Fathers have been described as the head, concerned with vocational and financial matters, encouraging the children to extend themselves beyond the family, and preparing them for roles in society.

Associated with these stereotypes is the unfounded generalization that mothers are innately equipped to be the better parent. There is no support for the notion that mothers are better parents. Mothers have the innate ability to bear children (and some can breast feed infants). At that point, inherent gender differences stop. Both fathers and mothers can perform all instrumental roles associated with parenting.

Parenting can be viewed from many angles. One view emphasizes the parents' biological and genetic contributions. Your children will grow to resemble you physically, socially, emotionally, and intellectually. Another view emphasizes parents' legal responsibilities and rights. The law holds parents responsible for children's moral and social conduct. In turn, they have legally granted rights over their children. A third view emphasizes a parent's financial role. Childhood is a time of financial dependency. A parent's ability to provide a stable and sufficient income is assumed. Another view stresses social relationships between parents and children. This role was discussed in a previous section on the role of the family. A fifth view emphasizes the individual or psychological relationships a parent develops with each child. Parents see unique characteristics in each of their children and try to respond to each one differently. A personalized relationship develops which allows individual characteristics to flourish.

Thus, fathering includes any of these characteristics: biological, legal, financial, social, and psychological. The more roles the other assumes, the stronger his influence. For example, a father who only has a biological relationship with his children has less influence than a father who also has financial, social, and psychological relationships. Active fathering requires some participation in all realms.

Effective Parenting

Most men have learned to be fathers through on-the-job training. They probably never discussed how to be an effective father with their parents nor read a book on the subject. They became fathers overnight and gradually acquired a set of attitudes and behaviors which seemed to work.

Most approach fathering based on a combination of how their fathers acted, watching other fathers, seeing the effects of their actions, and using then common sense. They discover that being a parent is a complicated process. Techniques which seem to be effective with one child may not work with others. Sometimes it is amazing how the personality characteristics of two children from the same parents and raised in the same home can be so different. Some of the confusion about fathering may be removed by considering your role from a child's viewpoint.

Love Versus Hostility. Consider how your children would describe you along a continuum going from loving to hostile. This refers to the degree you love and value your children. Children who know a father values them highly and feel his deep love and affection would rate him highly on the love dimension. Children who feel a father rejects and dislikes them and treats them with disdain would rate him high on the hostility dimension. Children who sense a father does not strongly feel one way or the other would rate him toward the center.

Permissiveness Versus Restrictiveness. Consider, too, how you would be described along a continuum going from restrictive to permissive. This refers to the degree to which you exercise control over your children's daily decisions and actions, not to the methods used to exercise control. Children who see a father allowing them

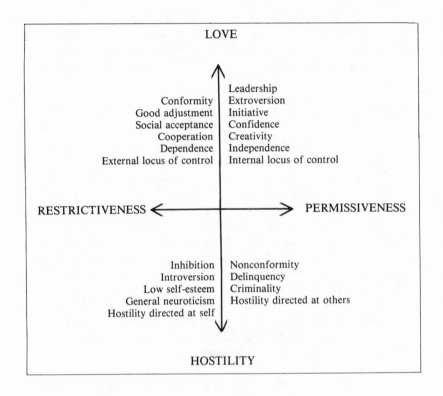

**Relationships among parent
behaviors and child outcomes**

wide latitude and autonomy in deciding what they can do and how they can do it would rate him strongly on the permissive side. On the other hand, children who view their father as allowing very little freedom to make decisions or carry them out would rate him strongly on the restrictive side. Again, children would rate their father toward the center when he did not favor one viewpoint over the other.

How would you rate yourself? You may want to ask your children to rate you, too. You may find that they see you as you see yourself. Don't be surprised, however, if they see you a bit differently.

How you behave does have an effect on children, as shown in the figure below. Children raised in a family characterized by love and restrictiveness tend to be well-adjusted, socially accepted, cooperative, dependent, and conforming. Children raised in a family characterized by love and permissiveness tend to be leaders, extroverted, confident, creative, and independent. Children raised in a family characterized as permissive and hostile tend to be nonconformists, delinquents, and hostile toward others. Children raised in a family characterized as restrictive and hostile tend to be inhibited, introverted, neurotic, low in self-esteem, and hostile toward themselves.

While there is no one right set of parental characteristics on which everyone would agree, well-adjusted and stable children tend to be raised in an atmosphere of love and warmth. Thus, if this is your goal, high ratings along the love dimension strongly suggest you may succeed.

The optimal location along the permissive-restrictive dimension is not so extreme and may be close to the center. The best parenting is neither permissive nor restrictive but consistently displays a more moderate position which includes setting realistic limits for children while allowing them meaningful choices within those limits.

Fathering Following Divorce

Children's well-being following a divorce is most strongly influenced by three factors. First, the strength of their own personality prior to divorce has a decided impact on their adjustment. Children who are happy, well-adjusted, and secure before a divorce are more likely to show those same traits following a divorce. Conversely, children who have weak personalities and feel insecure are more likely to have problems.

Having a stable, loving relationship with both parents also strongly influences children's adjustment. Children need to share the attention and affection of both their mother and father. Children who have access to only one parent or children who sense severe frictions between parents and are used as pawns in their parents' struggles also are at risk.

The third factor concerns the regularity and frequency of contacts with their father. When mothers have custody, the children's responses to divorce are more healthy when fathers have frequent and regular contact with them. Fathers who don't visit, phone, or write frequently and regularly are likely to find their children confused, angry, and lonely.

The third factor concerns the regularity and frequency of contacts with their father. When mothers have custody, the children's responses to divorce are more healthy when fathers have frequent and regular contact with them. Fathers who don't visit, phone, or write frequently and regularly are likely to find their children confused, angry, and lonely.

Most children initially are opposed to the divorce. Following the divorce they want their father to return to their family to assume his rightful place. They feel hurt and confused when this does not occur. However, they feel abandoned when their father is absent for a period of time. Thus, maintaining frequent and regular contact with children is central to their development. Moreover, this is central to the father's (and mother's) adjustment too. The importance of the father's role during and following a divorce is clearly established.

Ways to Help Your Children

As their father you have a central role in determining how your children will progress through this divorce. You may choose to flee, to leave the responsibilities for helping them to others—or to themselves. Hopefully, you not only will stay but will remain an active parent during this time when children need their father.

As parents, you and their mother know them best. Moreover, they look to you for information, leadership, guidance, and understanding. Friends, neighbors, and relatives also can be helpful. But your relationships with your children cannot be matched by others. While there is no formula to success, the following suggestions, when followed, will help children adjust to the stress and anxiety associated with divorce.

Strive for Consistency.   Everyone needs regularity in his life. Children are happiest and most content when they can count on their world to be run in an orderly fashion. Specific times for sleeping, eating, dressing, schooling, and other regular activities simplify their lives. Maintaining their home, friends, relatives, after-school and weekend activities also contribute to their stability. In general, children respond to divorce best when they are made to undergo few other changes.

Strive for Simplicity.   Sometimes divorced adults choose to overload their lives with activity to drown out the loneliness, sorrow, and pain. They also may inflict children with this harmful strategy. By scheduling every minute of their day they may feel they have acted responsibly. Overscheduling children with activities and responsibilities may alleviate adult anxieties while adding theirs.

A child who experiences only the stress of divorce will make it fine. A child who experiences stresses from a number of different sources seriously risks becoming disturbed and maladjusted. Keeping a child's world consistent and uncluttered serves to insure a healthy transition.

Keep Commitments.   A healthy transition also requires you to be dependable toward your children. Within this period of turmoil they need to trust in you.

Children will want to know what time you will pick them up from their mother's house, when you will get David's bike fixed, how long you will be away from the house on your date, and answers to a zillion other questions. Some questions cannot be answered. However, by giving accurate answers to those that can, you provide needed reassurance about their future.

By keeping these commitments you reassure them that you have integrity, that their trust in you is well-founded, that they can have faith that the long-term solutions to their problems will also occur.

Communicate with Your Children.   One of the most common problems wives find in husbands is their seeming unwillingness to communicate. Upon coming home from work, he may tune into the TV (often even through dinner), read the paper, take a nap, and do other solitary activities which act as barriers between him and his family. This pattern—or others which limit communication within the family—must be broken.

You must take time and exert the effort to talk with your children. The divorce and the children's future are only two of many topics which obviously need extended discussions. Discussions on less heavy topics also are needed: their school and academic work, sports and other interests, friends, current events. An interchange of your knowledge, thoughts, and feelings is crucial to understanding yourself and your children. This process will encourage the development of a more realistic picture, a better understanding of each other, and stronger commitments.

Communicating involves active listening and attention to what children say and how they say it. By occasionally rephrasing in your own words what your children say, you can test your own understanding. Communicating involves accepting and respecting your children's thoughts and feelings. By expressing a sympathetic understanding and being empathetic, you encourage your children to continue communicating their thoughts and feelings and to develop a closer understanding of other viewpoints. Your children will appreciate your interest in them, your willingness to share your thoughts with them, and your ability to listen to and to learn from their views. Your children's self-confidence will be enhanced as will their confidence in you. These qualities are indispensable to their adjustment.

Provide Love and Rules.   During times of divorce, children need the reassurance that comes from your loving them. Reassurance also comes from setting rules and standards for their actions. Fathers should take more responsibility for setting standards with younger children but should share that responsibility increasingly as children get older. Children are likely to interpret these behaviors as saying to them:

"I love you. You are a valuable person. And, like all well adjusted people, we need to follow some important rules. You don't need to be rule bound. In fact I encourage you to think for yourself. However, you have a responsibility to your family and society to obey those rules which generally insure our common welfare and happiness."

Children who receive such reassurances tend to be well-adjusted, leaders, and to accept and respect themselves and others.

Keep Children Involved with Other Relatives and Friends. Effective parenting actually involves a complex network of people who take an interest in your children. Grandparents, aunts and uncles, teachers, friends, neighbors, and baby sitters are but some of the people who take time to be with your children and influence their development. While mothers and fathers exert a strong force on children, the influences of others are no less real. Everyone remembers the love and guidance he received from a caring relative or teacher. You also remember those who were cruel and insensitive.

Divorce can be most traumatic on children who become isolated from other loving and caring persons. An only child who has no grandparents, aunts, uncles, or cousins nearby is likely to feel very lonely and isolated; to display strong dependency behaviors; and to experience other difficulties adjusting to the divorce. Adjustment is more rapid and complete when a child feels the concern and support from various relatives and friends.

Fathers need to insure that children's contacts with their extended family and friends continue, even increase, during this time. Recognize, too, that these people to whom you also look for support may be withdrawing. Thus, your strong initiative and a stiff upper lip may be needed to insure that your children remain involved with others who can provide love and care so necessary for them to receive.

Effective parenting involves screening others who come in contact with your children to insure that they protect your children's dignity, respect their rights, and are genuinely concerned with their welfare. Minimize contact with those who do not have a beneficial impact on your children. Carefully select baby sitters and inform them of their duties.

Keep in Touch with the Schools.   Schooling deserves particular attention. Fathers and teachers need to form a close working relationship to insure mutual understanding and support. Inform them of any school-related problems and ask them to call you periodically to report on your children's progress. Ask them to be aware of symptoms showing stress and emotional problems. Assume initially that your children's teachers are competent and caring. If you find this to not be true, discuss your concerns in a visit with the principal. The principal may have good ideas about alternative arrangements and may be willing to pair your children with just those teachers they need.

However, do not insist upon special privileges for your children because they are from a divorced family and thus have special needs. All children have special needs. School personnel are turned off by that attitude. They respond more positively to people who respect—not challenge—their authority and to invitations to work jointly with parents toward mutually agreed upon goals.

The school environment may affect the child's adjustment as strongly as the home environment. Having a predictable, structured school routine enables children to feel confident about themselves and others, to know what is expected, and to behave accordingly. The fighting and disruptions children often display during the separation and following divorce may soon end when a teacher provides a stable and consistent school program. The teachers and principal are interested in the welfare of each child and are likely to cooperate with you in sharing information and planning beneficial child-management strategies.

Be Aware of Neighborhood and Community Factors.   Children's closest friends tend to live near by and attend the same schools. Know something about them and their families. Discuss friendship qualities you look for in your friends and your children's friends. Help them to discern the good from the not-so-good. The standards you establish for your children's friends should match the standards you have for your friends.

Conclusion

Wide differences exist in how children respond to divorce. Some children do very well, while others experience a rash of problems.

In general, children have no serious long-lasting problems when stress arises only from the divorce. Children do have serious problems when stress arises from various sources. A father plays a vital role in anticipating problems, trying to prevent them before they arise, being aware of possible problems their children experience, responding to them personally, and getting professional help for them when necessary. An inactive father not only is unavailable to help his children directly but by his absence contributes to their problems. Hopefully, father will choose to remain active and to continue contributing to their children's recovery through this difficult time and beyond.

6

Child Custody

A Central Issue

Nancy Voigt Wedermeyer

The custody and visitation arrangements set up in the original divorce decree typically have a lasting effect on the future relationships between children and their divorced parents. Far too often, parents meekly follow that they believe is the standard arrangement without thinking through the meaning it will have for themselves or their children. There are many possible arrangements, and society's idea of what is best seems to be rapidly changing. Stability in daily life and continuing strong relationships with each parent clearly are important for children.

This chapter explains how custody and visitation traditionally have been arranged and why. Then, the three most common types of custody are described in detail, including reasons for choosing each type, difficulties with it, how to make it work well, and strategies for convincing the court to approve it. Six particularly thorny issues—continued contact between the parents, child support, geographical moves, holidays, making changes later on, and the role of the courts and the lawyer—are discussed separately. The theme of the chapter stresses the importance of thinking through all the issues and the positive outcomes that can occur for fathers who make the effort to set up the right situation for their own particular family. It is assumed that the primary goal of the father and mother is to make the post-divorce situation as positive for their children as possible.

WHAT HAS TRADITIONALLY BEEN DONE

The very use of the term "custody" reflects the historical roots of contemporary American laws. Child-custody laws can be traced back to Roman private law under which the father had the absolute right to control his children. This notion, carried over to English law in the 14th century, stated that the father had the right to his children's custody, because he supported them and hence deserved their services. There were no visiting rights for the mother, who herself was the property of her husband.

As Western society became industrialized, work became separated from the home. Also, children were kept at home longer and greater emphasis was placed on their needs for nurture and education. The woman's role in the family became one of meeting these needs. Near the mid-19th century, U.S law began to reflect these changes, and the absolute power of the father over the family was taken away and usually vested in women. Women were seen to have the right to continue motherly roles. Thus, child custody considerations still were determined in the light of parental rights. However, late in the 19th century, U.S. law began to take note of the rights of the child, a trend which was formalized with the guide line, "the best interests of the child," in 1925.

Just what arrangements will best suit the child's interest is an issue still open to interpretation. During the early 20th century the idealization of the wife/mother role continued. The influence of Freudian psychology helped to shape the legal "doctrine of tender years," which asserted that children under the age of 6 or 7 particularly needed to be cared for by their mother. State laws gave legal preference to the mother as custodian after divorce, especially during the child's tender years. Challenges to this practice were successful only when it was proved to the court that the mother was not fit to be a parent. With older children there might be some consideration of their wishes, or their need to live with a same-sex parent, as a model. The prevalent custody arrangement was to give the mother *sole* custody of the children, with the father allowed some visiting time. In some instances sole custody was *split* between the two parents, most often with sons being in the custody of the father and daughters in the custody of the mother. This model was developed in a social context in which divorce occurred only if one spouse defaulted grossly on his or her marital obligations.

American family life has been changing rapidly in the last 20 years. Well over half the mothers of school-age children are working outside the home and fathers are more involved at home with the children and household tasks. Psychologists are beginning to deny that the first 5 years of life are a critical period in which basic personality is determined. They are pointing out that growth is lifelong. Children need guidance throughout their childhood years, and both fathers and mothers have important contributions to make. In addition, adult experiences, responsibilities, and growth are being recognized as important in life-span development.

Finally, divorce has become fairly common. The passage of "no-fault" divorce laws in most states reflects acceptance of the fact that today marriages are dissolved because spouses just do not get along very well together although neither has been irresponsible to the marriage.

Accompanying these changes is a new type of custody arrangement called *joint* custody. Under the arrangement both divorced parents continue to be actively involved in the guidance of their children. The amount of time the children spend with one or the other parent varies widely according to circumstances, but neither divorced parent has the sole right to make major decisions concerning the child without consulting the other.

These three forms of custody—sole custody, split custody, and joint custody—are three basic ways in which to legally arrange parent-child relationships after divorce. Because family law is a state matter, the legal details will vary from state to state. In most states sole custody remains the legally preferred arrangement. Nearly half of the states have laws making it illegal to use the sex of the parent as a reason for awarding custody. However, when custody is contested, many of these states, together with most other states, still hold to the "tender years" doctrine, which favors the mother.

When custody decisions are arrived at by both parents, most state laws are flexible to allow parents to set up legally whatever provisions they believe are in the best interests of their children. Most courts will approve the parents' request, provided they are convinced that the request has been well thought out.

Each of the major custody types has different effects on parents and children. These should be considered in making decisions regarding custody. You will also need to know how to make the most of each situation and how to convince the court of its feasibility. These issues are considered next.

SOLE CUSTODY

In keeping with the idea that divorce ends the marriage with complete and final separation of the spouses, an award of *sole custody* gives one parent the full parental authority over the children. The custodial parent also assumes sole authority for the children. The noncustodial parent has no legal right to make any decisions concerning the child although he or she may have financial obligations to the custodial parent and children. The noncustodial parent typically is awarded legal rights to see the children. The time schedules for visiting may be specified by the divorce decree or left to the two parents to work out the details as they occur.

Reasons for Choosing Sole Custody

There are a number of reasons favoring sole custody. It tends to finalize the divorce because the custodial parent is legally free of obligation to consult the ex-spouse concerning the children. Marriage ties are more easily broken where there are fewer cooperative efforts and needs for collaboration. Also, when conflict between two parents is great, the legal denial of power to one may end the conflict. Proponents of sole custody also argue that the clear legal definition of custody/noncustody reduces the likelihood of the family returning to the court to work out details of the arrangement.

Sole custody has been seen as being good for children because they presumably no longer will be the center of the parental conflict. Parents who divorce are parents who disagree too strongly to live together. They cannot be expected to cooperate after the divorce. When one parent is guiding the children's lives, they will not have to deal with the contradictions or tension caused by parental differences. With sole custody there also is no question where the children's home is. They feel a sense of security based in living in one neighborhood with one set of friends and with one set of clothes and toys.

Sole custody may be favored by divorcing couples who had a strong division of labor during their marriage. A parent who has not been highly involved with the children on a day-to-day basis may not feel adequately prepared to undertake major parental responsibility. A parent who was almost totally involved in child rearing during the marriage may feel that losing that involvement—even part time—would be a loss of the meaningfulness in life.

Another attraction of sole custody is that one parent is freed of many parental responsibilities. Those wishing to divorce because of the feeling that family life is stifling, or those wishing to use the marital breakup as a stepping stone to a new life style will find child-rearing activities burdensome and would seek a noncustodial relationship with their children.

Finally, sole custody is the traditional pattern. Although there are increasing complaints against it, it is the most common and tested method for raising children following a divorce. It is generally agreed that most children have survived parental divorce without great disruptions in their development or becoming emotionally disturbed, and most of these children of divorce have grown up in sole-custody homes. Neighbors, employers, and in-laws are familiar and sympathetic with and supportive of sole custody.

Difficulties with Sole Custody

Parents without custody of their children tend to withdraw from their children's lives. This occurs frequently with fathers. Seeing their children infrequently simply makes the children seem less important and less central to their lives. For many fathers the continual short-term reunions and farewells may become so painful that they seek to avoid them. Four days a month of seeing your children may not seem sufficiently important to refuse a job promotion which requires a move to another city or state.

Parents and children who see each other infrequently and only under visiting circumstances tend to lose the sense of intimacy they used to have. The noncustodial parent typically is not available as crises arise when the children really need him or her and no longer can make important decisions concerning the children. Often the relationship deteriorates to a "perpetual honeymoon" in which the noncustodial parent always entertains the children for fear that they will be unhappy and reject the parent.

Various reasons lie behind the trend for many noncustodial parents to visit less and less frequently and to stop making financial support payments after the first year or two following divorce. Even parents who struggle to continue to be involved often express a bitterness to their children caused by the resentment of having to pay for the children without having any say as to how the money is spent or what happens to their children. Many fathers correctly feel they are excluded from having a central and important role in their children's lives.

The withdrawal of the noncustodial parent has several very negative effects. The most critical effect is the child's sense of abandonment. Most emotional disturbances in children of divorce center around their anger at being left, or their sense of being unlovable because a parent did not love them enough to stay. This sense of loss is particularly acute when the children have been close to the noncustodial parent before the divorce, or when the parent stays in the same geographic area but does not keep up—or is not allowed to maintain—the relationship with the children.

Secondly, the withdrawal of the noncustodial parent increases the burden of the parent with custody. The typical custodial parent is a woman with low-level-job skills. Without independent financial support and time to herself, she becomes pressured and less able to care adequately for the children. Many problems children experience are related more to the post-divorce stress of the single parent than to the divorce itself.

A third important effect is the loss of one parent as a role model of a particular sex. A large amount of research literature indicates that boys who live in father-absent homes are less adept at typical masculine skills, such as working with numbers, and that girls who grow up without fathers have difficulty learning how to relate appropriately to men. Little evidence has been collected on growing up in homes without a mother.

When the noncustodial parent does not withdraw, problems still can persist. The all-too-typical honeymoon relationship with the noncustodial parent places a strain on the child's relationship with the custodial parent. Teaching a child self-discipline or responsibility around the home is more difficult when the child resists guidance with statements such as "At Mommy's house, I never have to make my bed or do the dishes."

Another type of loss is beginning to be recognized. This is the loss of the child to the parent. Fathers have become more actively involved with their children during the last 20 years, and they are less willing to routinely accept being removed from their children's lives. Fathers' rights groups have been organized in most states to protest their not being allowed to experience the personal growth found in caring for and being with their children.

Lastly, sole custody with "reasonable" visitation often is undertaken without any particular thought. It is accepted as the normal thing to do, and later implications are not thought out. Noncustodial fathers with legal rights to "reasonable visitation" frequently are prohibited from seeing their children by the custodial parent. Yet, upon seeking a court order to assure visitation by specifying visitation times, they are told that that constitutes a change of custody, and they first must prove that circumstances are different from those at the time of the divorce in order to change the original decree. Given the difficulty and expense involved in changing court orders, many fathers just give up. Thus, the original divorce agreement should be thoughtfully prepared.

How to Make Sole Custody Work

The strength of sole custody lies in the stability it provides. It clearly ends the partnership of marriage by giving one parent full authority to organize the children's lives. It requires that the children adjust to the demands of only one parent. It allows the children to develop roots in the lifestyle of that parent, and it frees the other parent to develop a more childfree life style. The weaknesses of sole custody are that it lessens the bond between the noncustodial parent and children and tends to overburden the custodial parent. The children typically recieve less care, both psychological and financial, and one parent is deprived of the value of raising children. The best way to handle sole custody situations is to emphasize the strengths and protect against the weaknesses.

Supporting regular and consistent contact between the child and the noncustodial parent is critical. This both supports the bonds between the children and the noncustodial parent and relieves some of the burdens on the custodial parent. If at all possible, the parents should arrange the visiting so that each child spends some special time alone with each parent.

If the parents live in the same city or fairly close by, they should agree upon a schedule—1 or 2 days a week, every other weekend, or whatever visiting arrangements seem right to them—and to schedule their other obligations around these fixed times. Time with the children must come before anything else. With younger children the predictability of the visits adds substantially to the child's sense of security. A set routine reduces the accidental loss of visiting time through confused schedules. It also minimizes contact between the parents since there is no need to continually negotiate arrangements. Finally, establishing visiting routines lessens the honeymoon effect, because, with visits occurring regularly, the noncustodial parent feels less need to court the children with favors. When parents live further apart, regular contact can be maintained by phone or letter. A child of 5 can fly by himself on a flight which does not require a change of planes. At 8 he can change planes, too.

As children approach adolescence they will want more say in determining the visitation arrangements. Typically they are more interested in spending time with their friends than with either parent. An older child also may wish to change the custody arrangements. This may come from a curiosity to see what it would be like to live with the other parent, or a fear of losing contact with the other parent. Many parents who allow their adolescent children to move to the noncustodial parent have found that this helps children to resolve their feelings about the divorce. If this move is allowed, it is important that the children can move back to the custodial parent if the new arrangements do not work out .

Maintaining regular financial support to the custodial parent is an important way to foster positive sole custody. Various expenses and strains are involved in caring for the child. Easing the burdens of the caretaker improves the situation for the child. Although paying money to someone who spends it in ways you disapprove of is very frustrating, it is worse for the children to labor under a strain caused by inadequate finances. Even elementary-school-age children show signs of anxiety over their family's financial insecurities. Also, young adults who have grown up in single-parent, divorced families stress the importance of knowing that another caring parent is there. Withholding money to spite an ex-wife often produces greater and more lasting damage to the children.

Perhaps the greatest difficulty facing noncustodial parents is the background nature of their role. Typically the law strips them of all important decision-making powers. This tends to be very difficult on men who thrive in positions of authority and self-control. Children often do not recognize and appreciate this difficulty until they near adulthood themselves. But then the patient care and giving-ness of the background parent pays off in a full adult-child/parent relationship.

When a parent chooses to disappear rather than play a background role, the custodial parent needs to help the children confront and work through the issue of being abandoned. Pointing out how terrible the parent is to have left does not help a child who is asking, "Am I so terrible that even my own parent doesn't want to be with me?" Children need reassurance that the parent left for his or her own reasons, not because of them. Children also need to develop and rely upon other sources of self-esteem—friends, siblings, and other relatives who accept and value them. All of us benefit from such reassurance, but children who feel abandoned by a parent have a critical need for this.

Little has been said so far concerning the sex of the custodial parent. Despite equal-rights laws, the society and the courts are biased and favor the mother as custodian when there is sole custody. Yet, research clearly shows that fathers can be as capable as mothers in caring for their young children as well as those of older ages. However, such evidence typically is not considered by or known to a court strongly steeped in tradition. Recognizing the fitness of the father as custodian typically means judging the fitness of both parents. When both parents want to continue to be actively involved as parents, sole custody probably is not the best choice.

How to Obtain Sole Custody Legally

Laws governing divorce vary from state to state. Thus, it often is necessary to hire a local attorney and to do some studying on your own to determine how to comply with the particular laws of your state. Most courts will approve an agreement presented jointly by the parents if it appears sensible. An uncontested joint request for sole maternal custody will probably be accepted without question. Even when parents present a joint agreement, the court may request that the reasons be clearly demonstrated if sole paternal custody is requested. Sole custody generally is the preferred arrangement.

The court typically expects the mother will be the custodian. Fortunately many fathers are successfully challenging this tendency and are being awarded sole custody of their children. The fitness of the father and the desire of both parents to agree to the decision are the most important points to prove.

When the two parents disagree about who should have sole custody, the fitness of each parent will be judged and will be the sole issue in states and localities in which mothers are not given preference. Given equal fitness between the two parents, the mother most likely will be given custody, no matter what the state law says, due to the lingering societal prejudice that taking care of the children is really a woman's role. Thus, in contested cases where fathers want custody, they must present a well-documented case of their fitness and deficiencies in the mother.

When both parents want to continue a close relationship with their children after divorce, and each is fit to have custody, some form other than sole custody should be considered.

Most importantly, realize that the original decree has the force of law, and courts are very reluctant to make changes. The typical requirement for making a legal change is to show a *material change in circumstances*. A request to change a custody or visitation because of a change of parental opinion or thoughts typically will not be honored by the court. In the midst of divorce proceedings it sometimes is tempting to accept the first compromise offered and get it all over with, but arrangements concerning the children are too important to be treated lightly. Your relationship with your children probably involves the longest-lasting aspect of the divorce decree. The decree governs parent-child relationships until the child is an adult. Your relationship with them now and over the years will have a decided impact on your happiness and theirs. Your decision and its effect will be life-lasting. Try to work out arrangements which will achieve what you want for yourself and them over that full time span.

SPLIT CUSTODY

A divorcing couple having more than one child may wish to consider the option of *split custody*. This means dividing the children and granting each parent sole custody of one or more of the children. Each custodial parent maintains all parental rights and obligations for the children living with him or her and acts as a non-custodial parent toward the children living with the ex-spouse. Parents often choose a split custody arrangement whereby the boys go with the father and the girls go with the mother. However, other arrangements also are workable.

Sometimes split custody occurs after a sole-custody arrangement proves unsatisfactory. One child may choose to move to the other parent's house, and a legal change is instituted. Split custody is a legal term. Only when the change becomes legal does the parent gain custody provisions.

Reasons for Choosing Split Custody

Since split custody is really sole custody for each of the parents, it has some of the same advantages of sole custody. It formally breaks many provisions of the parenting partnership. It allows the child the stability of a single home and a single set of parental guidelines. It also has several other potential benefits. Neither parent is totally denied the continued experience of raising his or her children. Nor is one parent given the total burden of responsibility for the couple's children. Where there are many children, sharing of the responsibilities may be quite important. Also, parents who choose split custody often have specific reasons for their choices about which children will go with which parent. The choice might recognize a special bond between one child and one parent, keep apart a child and parent who do not get along, recognize a child's preference, or be based on the belief that a child will develop a more appropriate sexual identity by living with a parent of the same sex.

Difficulties with Split Custody

Most of the advantages of split custody appear to benefit the parents while most of the difficulties affect the children. The greatest difficulty is that the children lose close contact with their brothers or sisters in the custody of the other parent. Sibling relationships are generally important. Experience has shown that they can be particularly important forms of support and comfort to children affected by divorce. This is particularly true when there are two or three children close in age and interests. Where there are more than three children of widely different ages, this may not be such an important drawback.

One of the potential strengths of split custody is that the parents may pair the child with a particular parent for special reasons. This may backfire, however. The child may not ask—"Why was I chosen by this parent?"—but rather—"Why did my other parent want my brothers but not me?" This might increase the child's sense of abandonment and sibling rivalry and jealousy. Also, children who live only with family members of the same sex develop fewer skills and greater doubts about their ability to get along with the opposite sex. Sibling rivalries also may be increased by financial, managerial, housing, clothing, and other differences between the two homes. The children with a parent who makes less money and has a lower standard of living may feel shortchanged and resentful.

Split custody also sacrifices some of the benefits of sole custody. Neither parent is freed for the personal growth available without the responsibilities of child rearing. Yet, both parents feel the loss of a primary bond with at least one of their children. Lastly, split custody is not likely to receive wholehearted support from neighbors, teachers, in-laws, employers, or the courts. People are apt to assume that the parents' motivation was primarily a power struggle and to be critical of them for denying the children a unified home. Parents may be accused of treating children like property. The division of children is viewed as the division of property between man and wife.

Few divorcing parents have chosen split custody. There is virtually no research information about it. One survey on custody and visitation arrangements did report that both parents and children from divorced families see split custody as being unsatisfactory. Even the few children who come from families with split custody do not advocate this arrangement.

How to Make Split Custody Work

Since split custody is a form of sole custody, many of the strategies considered in the previous section will help it work. Parents should arrange for specific and routine contact with the other children not directly under their care, and give each child individual time with each parent. The siblings should spend some time all together. When parents live close, the sibling visits might be arranged by letting all the children stay with one parent one weekend and with the other parent the next. Many parents also let the children spend summers together, half at one house and half at the other.

Since the children can be affected negatively by financial differences in split custody, the parents may wish to try to equalize the financial situation for the children. The parent with more money or fewer children may contribute child support to the other household. Another way is to keep track of direct expenditures on all of the children and have each parent pay a proportion of the total expense according to his or her earning power. This process tends to be unsuccessful since it requires a higher degree of trust and cooperation than most former partners are willing to show.

How To Obtain Split Custody Legally

As with sole paternal custody, split custody is different from the typical pattern. The court may approve it if both parents can convince the court that they support it and that they are clear about what they are undertaking. Again, the court will be interested in the fitness of each parent. Additionally, the court may want evidence about specific plans which allow the siblings to spend time with each other, and the criteria used in deciding how to split the children.

JOINT CUSTODY OR CO-PARENTING

Joint custody is a legal arrangement whereby neither divorced parent can make major decisions concerning the children without consulting the other parent. The division of the children's time between the parents can follow a variety of patterns. In some cases the child spends half a week in the home of each parent. In other cases the child may alternate weekly, every 2 weeks, every month, or every 6 months. Parents sharing custody of school-age children typically live in the same neighborhood so that the children exchange homes to eat and sleep in but keep the same school and friends. Sometimes, however, the parents live further apart, and the children either spend the school year with one parent and the summer with the other, or alternate entire years. Occasionally parents sharing custody have kept the children in the family home, and the parents alternate, one living with the children and the other living in a nearby apartment. At given intervals, the parents switch, with the one who had been at home taking over the apartment, and vice versa. Joint custody is sometimes called *co-parenting* by those who believe it is more important as an attitude than as a legal status. The term "custody" implies ownership, and proponents of co-parenting tend to believe that the parental relationship is very important and do not consider that any parent "owns" his or her child.

Reasons for Choosing Joint Custody

The growing popularity of joint custody is due to the increased involvement of fathers as parents and of mothers as members of the full-time labor force. Joint custody is also popular because of the changing nature of many divorces. Couples who decide to divorce because of general incompatiblity often part with fewer grievances and less motivation to hurt or punish the other through the children. In many cases, the couple explicitly recognizes that the marital and parental bonds are independent. The parents' wish to separate from each other does not require the children to be separate from them.

Co-parenting maximizes the continuity and normalcy of the child's relationship with each parent since both parents remain in frequent contact and retain responsibility for the child. Neither the parents nor children face a loss of parent-child relationships.

Difficulties with Joint Custody

Though much appears fair and reasonable in joint custody, a number of potential difficulties exist. Their seriousness cannot be judged since the trend toward joint custody is relatively new and little research exists. Most concerns are raised by people who favor sole custody as the appropriate arrangement. Testimony by parents who share custody generally is enthusiastic for the new pattern, but this does not necessarily mean that their way of handling things can be carried out successfully by others who are less idealistic or less able to cooperate with an ex-spouse.

A major concern is that parents who disagree strongly enough to require a divorce are poor risks for cooperative parenting. They may continue their conflicts with the children caught in the center as the parents interact around child-related problems. A related concern is that the cooperative parenting will be an excuse for the parents to stay in touch and even have some control over each other. They may never really finalize the divorce. Another major concern is that the children will be going between the two sets of parents and two homes "like a Yo-yo" and never develop a stable home life. Under these conditions children may attempt to play one parent off against the other as they go back and forth. Two separate parents may mean two separate sets of values and life styles with accompanying problems in defining right from wrong.

Two practical concerns relate to geographic mobility. Shared parenting is hard to maintain over geographic distances. A parent dedicated to continuing as an active parent after divorce may find it necessary to pass up job promotions or other attractive offers which require a move. Since each parent has legal custody, there may be fewer barriers to one parent legally taking the children to another state or country and suing for sole custody there.

Another potential difficulty arises from the cooperative nature of the arrangement. Children may form the idea that their parents' needs and wishes are being respected but theirs are not recognized. The children may demand that their wants and needs be recognized. This may result in children requesting to be with one parent more or receiving other special favors which could seriously jeopardize the joint custody agreement.

Joint custody is far from being generally accepted. Courts, acquaintances, relatives, and teachers are likely to be skeptical and nonsupportive. Fathers may be criticized for arranging to be with their children in order to be vengeful toward their ex-wives. Mothers may be criticized for giving up their natural maternal duties.

How to Make Joint Custody Work

Parents who choose to share parenting responsibilities for their children after divorce need to separate the marital and parental aspects of their relationship clearly. Restricting their communication to necessary matters concerning the children enables them to finalize the break in the marital relationships between themselves.

Another rule promoting success is, "live and let live." Arrange your home and life to be suitable to your needs and those of your children. Let their mother do the same. A degree of mutual respect is needed to avoid confrontations between the parents. Avoid talking with your children about what occurs at their other house if the intent is to elicit evidence which incriminates their mother or creates barriers between them and their mother. Parents should refuse to be manipulated if the children try to play one off against the other.

Joint custody directly involves at least three people and perhaps many more. To be successful, all people must cooperate first in setting up and then following a suitable schedule. Your children and their mother will rely on you to take over as an active parent at a particular time and place. By keeping your commitments, you create a good model for the others to follow. When obligations require a temporary change, confer with the children and their mother far enough in advance to minimize the inconveniences and, if necessary, to seek temporary child care elsewhere.

Joint custody often begins with a period of experimentation with the schedule of when and how much time the children are with each parent. Often schedules are adjusted toward longer blocks of time in order to minimize disruptions. Developing and sticking to a regular schedule appear to be very important. Maintaining the routine helps the children's sense of stability and their friends to be able to contact them. Schedules will probably be redesigned as the children get older.

As has been mentioned, shared parenting works most smoothly when both parents live in the same neighborhood. As children get older their peer relationships and own activities become more important to them, and they become less willing to give up these things to be with a parent. Some divorce decrees stipulate that both parents agree to stay in the same neighborhood and that, if one parent should move away, the remaining parent will gain sole custody of the children.

Joint custody seldom produces problems over money. Both parents usually are sincere in their willingness to continue to be responsible for the children and respectful of the other parent's similar sincerity. The result is that they do not hassle over money. Some parents follow a rule of paying for the child during the time when the child is at that parent's home. Others share the expenses proportionally according to their incomes.

Other practical matters, such as clothes or toys, are also handled in various ways. Many parents let the child have two sets of everything, one at each house. This clearly is preferable if allowed by the budget. Others pack everything up and transport it on moving day. A rule that a parent will not bring over any important and forgotten item helps to insure careful packing.

In deciding if you should seek joint custody, examine your parenting, job, social desires and requirements, and sort out priorities. They often are in competition. If you can put parenting and job requirements on about equal parity and your own social requirements much lower (particularly, when the children are with you), joint custody may work. If you have been an active parent since the children were small, joint custody may work. If you are trying to create a life which is in the best interests of the children (as well as yours), joint custody may work. If you are able and willing to assume major domestic responsibilities, joint custody may work.

How to Obtain Joint Custody Legally

Not all states have legal provisions for joint custody and many attorneys and judges are skeptical of it. Some may be persuaded by a careful presentation of statements by both parents. Sometimes the closest and most suitable arrangement may occur by assigning primary legal custody to one parent and allowing the chidren to spend equal time with each parent. A stipulation on visitation should be part of the divorce decree. However, often the parent themselves must monitor and enforce the jointness of their parenting. Courts willing to consider joint custody will be most interested in evidence concerning the fitness of each parent and specific plans for scheduling time so as to provide stability for the children.

It may be wise to protect the joint custody by specifying in the decree that a parent wishing to change the arrangement must prove a material change of circumstances in order to change the arrangement. Protection against the possibility of child snatching may be gained by specifying in the decree that neither parent may take the child from the state, except for specified vacations, without either written consent of the other parent or a court order.

Difficult Issues

A number of issues remain difficult no matter what the formal custody and visitation arrangements are. These include the nature of the continued contact between parents, financial child support, geographical moves, holidays, changing custody arrangements as the children grow older or the parents' situations change, and the role of the courts and the lawyer. Each issue will be discussed separately from the point of view of its effects on children.

Continued Contact between the Parents

A goal of divorce is for the parents to separate themselves from one another. Yet, the presence of children requires that they continue in some form of partnership until the children are grown. Even if one parent disappears entirely, the other parent must deal with the children's fantasies of that parent and their hurt, rejection, and emotions about being abandoned.

In divorce, children face two great dangers: to be abandoned by one parent and to be caught in the midst of parental hostilities. Parents can avoid both of these dangers by clearly separating their relationship with each other from their relationship with their children. They should restrict their communication to practical matters about the children and work to develop stable, routine patterns, in order to minimize issues requiring discussion. These principles can be followed using any of the three forms of custody.

Financial Support

Money has symbolic as well as practical importance in our society. People express themselves with their purchases and exercise control over others through finances. For one person to hand over money to be spent at the discretion of someone with whom he disagrees is very distasteful. Children's expenses are costly. Both parents can be expected to pay for their expenses. As a rule, the parent who has more money can be expected to contribute more. However, the contributions do not have to be proportionate. If you are earning more, you probably have more expenses. Child support figured on the basis of gross income tends to be unequitable. Increasingly, governments are tracking down and punishing parents who default on financial child support.

It has been noted that money seems somewhat less of an issue in joint custody situations. This seems to be because the parents have successfully shifted the focus away from their own differences to a shared concern for the child. This same spirit might be worked into the sole-custody models by allowing a noncustodial parent to pay directly for goods or services provided to the child. For example, the noncustodial parent may agree to pay for the children's clothing, medical care, and after-school child care while making minimal indirect support payments to the ex-spouse for housing and food costs.

Many fathers feel burned by two issues: exorbitant alimony and/or child-support payments and being deprived of time with their children. The two often go hand in hand. Many men must continue to provide support payments even when their spouse refuses to allow them to see their children. Resentment and animosity build. Under this situation a suitable resolution can occur by continuing support payments while resolving visitation and custody issues through the court.

Georgraphical Moves

Geographical distance greatly complicates the maintenance of close parent-child relationships after divorce. Greater distances add expenses of long-distance travel and telephone calls. It also makes informal, personalized, spontaneous contacts less feasible since trips usually must be planned ahead or around school schedules. Sharing friends and interest with a distant parent is more difficult. On the other hand, when one parent is not interested in maintaining a close relationship with children, geographic distance may help. Children who seldom see a parent who lives at a great distance can explain it as a problem of distance. Children who never see a parent who lives close by have few excuses to counteract the fear of being unlovable even by their own parent. Research clearly indicates that divorce is very hard on children whose parent lives close by but remains unseen and doesn't visit.

Parents may be wise to try to match geographical distance with their desire for closeness with the children. If a noncustodial parent expresses a desire through word or deed not to keep in close contact with the children, the custodial parent may find it helpful to move away. If the parents agree to share custody and one receives a particularly good job offer in a different city, the other parent may try to find a job there also. When a move increases the cost of maintaining contact with the child, it seems reasonable that the parent who made the move will assume some of the increased expense.

Holidays and Vacations

The lives of school-age children (and even young children of working parents) are highly affected by school schedules. On school and work days you have little choice about when to get up. Your early morning is a series of pressured moves toward being somewhere else, and most of your energies are used up in other settings before the family gets home again in the evening. In contrast, vacations and holidays provide for more relaxed time schedules, and activities are matters of choice. Also, many holidays have religious or cultural significance which is celebrated through rituals whose familiarity provides a sense of stability and roots. For many people these occasions are particularly thought of as family time.

A visitation or custody schedule in which children spend all the routine time with one parent and all the vacation time with the other contributes to the honeymoon effect. The household where you party and vacation is likely to seem more pleasant. In a similar way, people who work hard together often need a break together. Thus, a custodial parent and children who share their daily responsibilities also need to share some play time together. Holidays also are opportunities for extended families (grandparents, uncles, aunts, and cousins) to converge on one home. Children deserve the opportunity to develop the sense of familiar rituals and roots on both sides of their family.

Scheduling is an issue for all forms of custody and visitation. Reliable, cyclical schedules will contribute to your and the children's sense of stability and decreased confusion and turmoil. Planning some vacation time with each parent allows the children to know each parent in a better rounded fashion. Letting children regularly spend certain holidays with one parent and other holidays with the other may increase their sense of rootedness on both sides of the family. These kinds of schedules can be set up with any form of custody.

Making Changes in Custody Arrangements

The usual legal requirement for changing custody or visitation arrangements is to prove a substantial change of circumstances which makes the present arrangements no longer workable. Courts tend to require strong evidence that the change essentially destroys faith in the fitness of the original custodian. Even when the parents jointly agree on a request for a change, the courts may not treat it favorably because of their interest in upholding the stability of the original decision and the legal system. These facts in part explain the reluctance of courts to approve more creative custody arrangements: Judges often think that a situation which has not been thoroughly tried and tested probably is likely to be brought back to the court to be changed.

The courts' reluctance to make changes also points out the importance of establishing an original custody decree you can live with for a long time. Parents need to be careful not to let themselves be pressured to sacrifice long-term benefits such as plentiful visitation rights with their children and custody for short-term gains such as just getting the divorce over with.

As careful as you may be in tailoring the original decree, you or their mother almost certainly will want to change the decree at some later point. Thus, be prepared to go back to court. There are many possible reasons for a change. Few people realize the strain of being a single parent. One person has all the responsibilities and rarely receives a break or gets away. Some custodial parents must seek ways to enforce visitation to make the noncustodial parent give at least some care-taking relief. Thus, the custodial parent often seeks relief through a change in the decree.

Noncustodial parents often underestimate the degree to which they miss their children. Others increase their skills in doing household tasks and become more optimistic about being able to care for children. Some develop a satisfactory new life which makes them more willing to share themselves with their children. Also, joint custody arrangements sometimes are undertaken in a burst of idealism, and parents and children later find themselves unable to live up to their pledges.

The geographic move of a parent also causes a desire for change. A noncustodial parent who sees his children every other weekend may find a 2- or 3-week summer visit satisfactory. But if he does not see his children during the 9-month school year, he may wish increased time with them in the summer.

Children also may wish to make changes for a number of other reasons. When one parent remarries and has new children, the children of the first marriage may feel less welcome and wish to live with the other parent. Some children feel anxious about whether they still have a place in the new family and wish to live there to find out where they fit. After a long period of little contact with one parent, children may develop a fantasy about living with that parent. Also, children want more say in matters that affect them as they get older. Be prepared to accept that an older child may want to decrease visiting time with both parents in order to spend more time with friends.

As changes are likely to occur, parents should consider the possibility of making alterations in the divorce decree affecting visitation and custody plans set up at the time the original arrangements are made. Parents may choose to make flexible arrangements if they are confident that they can cooperate. Partners who lack mutual trust should spell out everything in writing. Most divorced families make changes as their needs change without ever going back to court. It is important to remember, however, that the court-ordered arrangements have the force of law, and courts are reluctant to make changes. Parents who feel they might have a future need for legal protection against changes should write the protections into the legal decree. Examples include the end to joint custody should a material change occur or a change in visitation patterns should one parent move out of the area. Hopefully, parents will accept a certain amount of flexibility in order to accommodate their children's changing needs.

The Role of the Courts and the Lawyer

The legal system can serve three important functions in divorce situations. Courts can be society's watchdog, protecting the weak. In this role it enforces the obligation of parents to continue to take care of their children (the weak) even after their marriage dissolves. Courts also function as mediators between hostile parties. When parents are truly stalemated, the court steps in as the decision maker and resolves the situation. In these situations the role of the lawyer is to protect his client from negative actions by the court or the other parent. In its roles as watchdog and mediator, the legal system steps in for parents who cannot or will not continue to provide for their children. The great majority of parents wish only to dissolve their marriage and not back down on their responsibility to their children. This seems especially true in no-fault divorce. For these parents the legal system serves in a third role, primarily that of a model, providing guidance and suggestions on how to carry out their continuing responsibilities appropriately.

We have discussed no-fault divorce. At the other extreme is the adversary system of divorce. In this system the marital partners become adversaries turning against one another in an attempt to prove that the other is responsible for the breakdown of the marriage. In no-fault divorce the spouses jointly agree to end the marriage, and there is no effort to assign legal blame for the divorce. Many divorcing parents today feel that a no-fault system should be extended to child custody. When parents divorce, it would be assumed that both parents will continue with caring responsibility for the children. The role of law would not be as a director-general preparing battle, but as a child advocate, encouraging parents to establish adequate care for their children. The law in some states is moving in this direction.

Most lawyers have been trained toward adversary perspective. If you prefer to use the adversarial approach to divorce, find the best lawyer you can to help you win. If you and your spouse want to avoid a battle, don't select a lawyer who is a fighter. Many men and women are paying the price now for letting two hungry lawyers involve them in a needless adversary battle that stripped them of their self-respect, property, and children. Divorce to most lawyers means a good healthy battle and money. Fathers also need to remember that lawyers have been taught that the maternal sole custody model is traditional and legally dominant. Select a lawyer who will support whatever arrangements you request or seek a mediation service.

CONCLUSION

Child custody is perhaps the most difficult area of divorce because the separating spouses cannot really close the door on the marriage as long as they continue to be in contact over the children. Adequate psychological nourishment of children requires continuity in important relationships and stability. Both of these are threatened by divorce, because the family life is reorganized, and the parents must separate themselves from one another. Careful consideration of options concerning custody and visitation can help parents to minimize the difficulties for themselves and maximize their responsiveness to the needs of their children.

7

Basic Legal Issues
Before You Begin
Edwin Terry, Jr.

Men going through a divorce are experiencing one of the most traumatic periods in their lives. Only the loss of a partner through death is more traumatic. For men with children or substantial property, the way divorce is handled literally shapes the course of the rest of their lives. This is a time when emotions can run high and irrational aspects of both partners' personalities overrule common sense and logic. Even the most sensible person who always seems in control can be consumed by fear, hurt, and a desire to inflict injury on his or her spouse. These are natural human emotions and probably cannot be overcome. However, there is much a man can do to prepare himself for what lies ahead.

ALTERNATIVES TO DIVORCE

More than half of the couples who separate later reunite and do not divorce. They hold open the option that there are alternatives to divorce. While their differences are severe and problems abound, they may wisely try various solutions to resolve their differences. Divorce becomes the last alternative.

Counseling is an effective method of settling marital problems for some. Therapy must involve both partners who meet regularly with the counselor. The husband and wife may meet the counselor separately in addition to their all meeting together. Both partners must be committed to make the marriage work for marriage counseling to be effective. Counseling may be done by a minister, a social worker, or a psychologist. In choosing a counselor, as in choosing a lawyer, careful selection is important. Pick a counselor who specializes in working with adults having marital problems, preferably someone who is known for his or her success in rebuilding marriages.

Mediation is a new and exciting alternative to the traditional marriage counseling. The basic idea underlying mediation is that a couple agrees to visit a mediator for a set number of sessions in an attempt to work out their problems. An impartial mediator should have a sound background in basic legal and financial principles along with skill in dealing with interpersonal relationships. After an open and candid discussion of the good and bad qualities affecting their marriage, the mediator and couple draw up a list of issues which forms the basis of their work plan. The mediator typically takes up one issue (e.g., finances) each week and attempts to deal with that issue alone. Other issues are pursued in subsequent sessions. Thus, mediation is an attempt to identify the separate issues pulling a marriage apart and to help the couple systematically overcome specific areas of disagreement and frustration.

Annulment is another alternative to divorce. The grounds for annulment vary from state to state and are usually quite narrow. They include insanity, fraud, impotence, marriage under the age of consent, and marriage while under the influence of alcohol or drugs, durress, or force. In addition, state statutes often require that a person not live with a spouse after these factors are discovered.

Trial separations are popular—sometimes even mandatory—in some areas. These arrangements in reality provide a cooling-off period for the couple to let passions subside and reason prevail. Both the husband and wife often realize that living apart produces major problems which may be more severe than those encountered in the marriage. Some men or women find a short fling away from the family an awakening experience and return with a greater commitment to make it work. During an extended separation the courts typically make orders concerning custody, visitation, and child support.

Types of Divorces

Ideally all appropriate avenues to resolve differences have been considered. However, alternatives to divorce for many do not work. When the decision is made to seek a divorce, you must decide how this will be handled. The old saying—"When all else fails, punt."—must *not* be followed. The new motto becomes—"When all else fails, maintain control of the ball." Do not relinquish your control and authority to anyone else—your wife, your lawyer, your children, or family. Keep the ball and control the game plan.

Deciding on the type of divorce you prefer is a major concern. There are two basic types of divorces in most jurisdictions. An uncontested or agreed divorce is the simplest type. A contested divorce is at the other end of the spectrum. Many divorces initially are uncontested but evolve into contests. Likewise, some that appear to be highly contested are settled after only a few hours of negotiation.

The truly uncontested divorce is a relatively recent development. States traditionally have granted divorce only when the parties were in conflict and one could prove adultery, cruelty, or other serious offenses. Many states now provide for a "no-fault" divorce. This has greatly encouraged the growth of the uncontested divorce.

What is an uncontested divorce, and when can one best use it? An uncontested divorce means exactly what the name implies—that the parties have agreed on the terms of their divorce and there is no need for a lengthy contested hearing. An uncontested divorce is particularly attractive because of its relative ease and economy. At least one state lets persons who have recently married and have no children and little property obtain an uncontested divorce outside the traditional legal channels. Often only one lawyer is involved in preparing the necessary papers. An uncontested divorce is a reasonable solution to untying the knots when there are no children or large property holdings.

However, if you have children or property, seek a lawyer. Obtaining "legal advice" from a co-worker or friend who has recently been though a divorce can be an expensive proposition and can lead to lifelong mental and emotional trauma. These "barbershop'' lawyers are most willing to provide legal advice and interpretations of the law on such matters as the "standard amount" of child support or alimony, the "customary" provisions regarding visitation, the way judges always give women everything they want, and the prospects for fathers getting child custody. Making decisions as to how both partners share in the division of financial liabilities and assets—and especially children—requires knowledge of the law and guidance for the future.

You and your wife may choose to use one lawyer when you are able to decide on most of the important matters. However, even if you and your spouse agree on all issues, it is always a good idea to obtain your own legal counsel. Ask your lawyer to review the proposed settlement, to answer those difficult questions you did not want to raise in the presence of your wife and your joint lawyer, to suggest ways to improve your settlement, and to propose ways to insure that the settlement, once arrived at, remains settled.

The use of your wife's lawyer to simply draw up the papers has been the downfall of many a divorced husband. Don't be surprised to discover that your wife selected the lawyer because of the lawyer's biases in favor of women and that she had prior contact with the lawyer to insure a favorable leaning toward her. You should assume that her lawyer is working for her, not the both of you. Use her lawyer only when there are no children or property involved.

An uncontested divorce also can be achieved when you both retain your own lawyers and provide tight and specific guidelines to them regarding the settlement and your preferences for resolving existing differences.

An uncontested divorce requires that both parties willingly resolve major differences with a degree of trust and faith in one another. However, at the same time, you must be informed, be prepared, and be willing to insist that your needs be met.

A contested divorce is the more traditional method of obtaining a divorce in the United States. Typically, both parties are represented by their own attorneys, and the case is decided either by a judge, a jury, or the two parties themselves out of court. This involves the classic adversary system, the foundation of the Anglo-American jurisprudence. Each party hires an attorney to represent his or her own interest. The lawyer, rightly or wrongly, must do everything in his or her power to see that the client's best interests prevail in the lawsuit regardless of what is "fair" or "just." Justice and the law are not necessarily synonymous. As the name implies, a divorce becomes a contest.

A contested divorce has both advantages and disadvantages. When both parties are represented by competent attorneys, the contested divorce insures that both parties are informed of their legal rights and obligations and are guided wisely toward a resolution. The contested divorce does not necessarily produce a bitter court fight. Often the lawyers can persuade clients with unreasonable or fanciful expectations to settle their differences in an amicable manner. The contested divorce taken to trial also offers the advantage of having a supposedly impartial observer—the judge or jury—make a decision that the parties cannot make themselves.

There also are several disadvantages to a contested divorce. Surprisingly, the contesting parties seldom get what they want. When a divorce is not settled amicably by the parties, the arbitrary decisions by judge or jury, especially in regard to children and property, tend to leave both sides dissatisfied. The judge or jury is not aware of all important and fine details which you strongly value. The matter for them is routine, while for you it is of great importance. Rancor and bitterness are the usual residue of a bitter custody right and affect both the parties and their children for the rest of their lives. In child custody fights the person granted custody often withholds visitation with the children from the noncustodial parent. The father who loses his children often is angry and bitter not only at his former wife but also at the judge, jury, and either or both of the lawyers. The loss of children is a frequent and distressing by-product of the adversary system.

THE LAWYER

The lawyer's role can be crucial in any divorce action. More care should be taken in choosing a lawyer if your divorce is more complicated. If you are involved in an uncontested divorce and have no children or important property, you generally can get by with the same lawyer who will draft the papers and go to court for a nominal fee. Advertising lawyers or a legal clinic are good choices as they tend to charge lower fees. For the cut-rate divorce, consult one of a number of books available at a book store that provide forms and step-by-step directions a person follows to do his own divorce. This latter method is followed only by the foolhardy.

If you are involved in a divorce which includes children or important property, get a lawyer. You and your wife may decide to find a lawyer to represent you both. This is understandable and often works well. Nevertheless, you also need to consult someone who can advise you more openly of your rights and the possible perils and pitfalls along the path you are following. Consulting another lawyer for advice is not a form of deception. It is a sign that you want to make the best decisions based on complete information and a consideration of your options and those of your wife.

As a man, be sure you have a good lawyer with experience in family law. A woman frequently can win with a lawyer of lesser abilities because traditional roles and prejudices strongly favor her position. A man, to win, must be more alert, prepared, and better represented. Having a lawyer with skill and experience to represent you in a vigorous manner is a key to your winning.

But how do you select a lawyer? Often the man goes to his attorney who represented him in the past in everything from wills to real estate. Unless this lawyer devotes a substantial portion of his practice to family law, find one who does. Important matters require a specialist, someone who has particular knowledge and a record for winning.

People find good family lawyers in various ways. Advice from others is a frequent method. Ask your friends who have been through a divorce about their lawyer—his ability to communicate, his rapport with people, especially with the judge, his knowledge of the law, his leadership in preparing for the case, his availability, and the bottom line—does he win cases. Information from others would represent the starting place in your search for the best legal advice.

The lawyer who represents you on general matters is a better source of information. There is an information network among lawyers which allows one lawyer to assess the abilities of others.

Ask your lawyer who he would get to represent him if he were in your shoes. Again, emphasize the importance of finding someone actively involved in a family-law practice.

Some states have family-law specialists certified by the state bar associations and listed separately in the yellow pages. These are good potentials. Another fertile source to identify competent lawyers is through your local men's legal rights organizations. Their referrals often are based on the attorneys' past experiences in winning divorce actions.

After you have the names of three or four lawyers, call each for an appointment. Face-to-face contact with a lawyer is the only practical method of hiring one. The initial consultation generally is not expensive and may be free. The initial consultation gives you the opportunity to size up the lawyer in his or her office. Keep notes on the information each provides and your responses to them.

How to use a Lawyer

A client and lawyer must cooperate to win a lawsuit. There must be a continuous exchange of information and a sharing of responsibilities. While your lawyer should give you the benefit of his expertise and advise you on legal matters, it is essential that you make the important decisions. For example, while a lawyer can advise you on the legal issues of child custody, you should decide the form custody should take and instruct your lawyer to represent this position.

To be effective your lawyer must know the facts of your particular case. Do not be afraid to burden him with facts you consider to be insignificant. He should be the judge of what facts he wishes to utilize in a particular case. Likewise, do not be afraid to tell him things, like past affairs, that you think may hurt your case. Nothing is more disconcerting to a lawyer than to learn damaging evidence about his client through the cross examination of all the facts relating to your case—good, bad, or indifferent. This will help him maximize your opportunities to win and minimize your chances to fail.

Your lawyer, if effective, is busy and may not attend to your case with the regularity and care you desire. Some divorces go on for months because the opposing lawyers are inefficient. Do not accept a slow and sloppy performance. You are paying for quality services. Expect them to perform. Nudge and, when necessary, prod your lawyer into action. The notion that the squeaky hinge gets attention prevails here, too.

Paying the Bills

Divorces can be extremely expensive. The complexity of issues and their ease of resolution generally determine a lawyer's fee. Most divorce lawyers charge by the hour. The charges can range anywhere from $40 per hour to $200 per hour. The lawyer will typically require a retainer, to be paid in advance, which serves as a deposit for work he expects to do. Expect to be billed periodically for the lawyer's services. Keep in mind that he will bill you for all the time he spends on your case—phone calls, conferences with the opposing lawyer, research, and correspondence—in addition to actual court time. Be sure you are fully aware of his charges, and have an estimate of the entire fee. You can minimize the costs of divorce by deciding issues amicably with your wife and by compromising on others.

PROBLEMS AND PREJUDICES IN THE LEGAL SYSTEM

Since the beginning of this century mothers usually have been awarded sizable finances and custody of children automatically unless there were significant and particularly objectionable defects in their character. Until recently, the situation has changed very little. Now, however, we are witnessing a rapid change in awarding alimony and custody. Fathering is being seen in a new light. While your important economic role has been recognized, your contributions to the family's social, emotional, and physical well-being are now being seen as well. Men who have been active participants in their families prior to divorce often want to continue their active roles following divorce. The liberalizing of traditional roles for women, especially the rapid increase in the number of women working, has helped change this picture. Now, more and more courts are beginning to take a more balanced view of custody and property settlements.

However, this does not imply that in divorce the legal system is equitable toward men. Although in theory the laws of a particular state may mandate equal treatment for both men and women, in practice this remains the exception rather than the rule. All things being equal, women still are granted custody of minor children, especially minor female children. The mother also is more likely to receive a larger share of the property, to be the beneficiary of alimony and other long-term financial compensations, and to have her legal fees paid by her former husband.

While the emerging attitudes during the last few years make it possible for some men to have the opportunity for a fair hearing, many lawyers either refuse to recognize this fact or choose to ignore it. This appears to be especially characteristic of older and more traditional lawyers practicing in conservative or rural areas. If your lawyer indicates that you have no opportunity to win your case, get a second opinion. While your first lawyer may be correct in his assessment of the case, it is prudent to solicit another counsel's advice. Lawyers, like judges and juries, are prone to go along with things "the way they've always been." Frankly, some have not kept up with newer statutes and are unaware of prevailing social changes.

While you may seek support and reassurance from all sources, the judge in a non-jury case is the only person whose opinion really matters in a divorce. The greatest lawyer in the world will not help one iota if the judge is bound and determined to rule for the woman. Judges develop reputations for the way they rule. A properly informed lawyer will know these tendencies and will have several alternatives for overcoming this obstacle. First, try to hire a lawyer who is extremely close to the local judges. Former judges who now are in private practice are often good candidates. Many female lawyers can be particularly strong in representing men. While this may sound cynical to some, it is often a most effective tool. Lawyers often can forum shop—that is, choose the presiding judge. If several judges are available and one tends to be more open to the rights of men, the lawyer should attempt to see that the case is tried before that judge. Recently divorced and younger judges tend to be particularly sensitive to the rights of husbands and fathers. If these options are not open and you have a difficult case, a jury may be the answer.

Presenting your case before a jury offers both advantages and disadvantages. It allows one to circumvent a particular, prejudiced judge. It also allows one to profit from the general public's fear and prejudice. For example, while a judge might not be shocked at the fact that your wife occasionally drinks too much or uses drugs, a jury might well decide custody on such an issue. A jury may be swayed by sympathy to offer a more favorable verdict than the judge.

A jury trial also has its problems. In many jurisdictions the wait for a jury trial can be lengthy—as long as 1 or 3 years. The emotional strain on you, your wife, and children often is severe. In addition, jury trials are very expensive. If you have a solid case that appears winnable, a good lawyer, and an impartial judge, then a jury trial is unnecessary.

8

Untying the Legal Knots

Preparing for a Divorce

Edwin Terry, Jr.

Divorce is a new experience for most men and women. While you may have observed friends and relatives going through this, now you are the participant. You will encounter a host of problems for the first time and will often be unsure of how to deal with them.

Your quest to untie and restructure legal relationships is furthered by recognizing that every divorce involves at least three parties: you, your wife, and the law and legal profession. Your involvement and that of your wife is obvious. The involvement of the law and legal profession, though obvious, is not always well understood. Yet, of the three parties, the law and legal profession may play the most active role in determining the outcome of the divorce. The legal decisions will affect your family and money and may affect your career, your place of residence, and other areas of your daily life. The decisions you or your wife make have little weight until they meet the approval of the court. You cannot avoid the legal system.

Prepare yourself for legal action as soon as you realize the possibility of a divorce. Most men mistakenly wait until they are sure a separation or divorce will occur. This is too late. Preparation for legal action will help insure your ability to act decisively and to influence events. Your success is likely to be vital to your future well-being and happiness and to that of your children.

PREPARING YOURSELF FOR LEGAL ACTION

When marital problems arise and divorce is at least a possibility, consult an attorney. Although one might not be ready to file, advance preparation is important to any lawsuit, especially a divorce. If you are well prepared, the odds for a favorable outcome improve immeasurably. The lawyer can help you assess your situation and recommend a course of action for your particular circumstances.

For example, he or she may advise you on the necessity of spending as much time as possible with your children if you intend to go for custody. Some men stay away from home when facing marital difficulty. This can devastate attempts to gain a suitable outcome on various issues, particularly, on child custody. Advice on preparing financial matters is also crucial. Many a husband has found himself in dire financial straits at the time of divorce because his wife planned better than he. You may be advised to minimize your earnings, to encourage your wife to gain or improve her employment, to eliminate joint savings and checking accounts, to buy expensive clothing, accessories, and a new car, and to protect yourself in other ways from unscrupulous actions by your wife or her lawyer.

If you and your wife are unable to agree on important matters and a contested divorce becomes inevitable, the most important actions a man can make are to plan ahead and to act first. Advanced planning allows you to chart the course for your legal action and to choose from among the many alternatives those best suited to your needs and those of your children. By acting first you can control the timing and gain tactical advantage. To let someone take your family, home, and money bespeaks not of your virtue but your stupidity and lack of planning. You, rather than your wife, can be in possession of the funds, living in your home, and providing the support and guidance your children need—not only now but in the years to come.

Many jurisdictions provide for temporary hearings to determine such matters as custody, visitation, support, and possession of the home. These *pendente lite* hearings often are crucial to future custody arrangements. Two somewhat competing notions prevail at these hearings. One is to establish rules to live by until a final settlement is made. These rules are seen as temporary. The other notion is that judges prefer consistency and are unlikely to alter rules that seem to be working. Thus, do not treat these initial hearings lightly. In fact, their outcome is likely to influence the final settlement strongly. Through careful planning and acting first, you can obtain temporary custody of the children. Having temporary custody greatly increases your chances of gaining final custody. By taking the offensive and perhaps catching your spouse unprepared, your chances for success on all matters are improved. Your witnesses will be ready for the hearing, your finances will be in order, and you will be in control emotionally. While this course of action may sound cynical and perhaps somewhat cruel, a contested divorce is just that—a contest. Enter the contest prepared to shape events toward the best interests of you and your family.

GROUNDS FOR DIVORCE

There are two types of grounds for divorce. The traditional grounds include adultery, mental cruelty, abandonment, living apart, conviction of a felony, or other major violations of a generally accepted civil and moral character. A divorce granted under the traditional grounds requires one spouse first to allege and then to prove the fault. This process produces bitter feelings and often is unnecessary.

A more recent trend is to grant divorce on grounds that do not specify some type of wrongdoing or fault. *No fault* and *unsupportability* are but two names given to this type of divorce. The granting of a divorce on these grounds recognizes the reality of modern life that some persons simply do not wish to live together as husband and wife. To require one spouse to plead or prove adultery or some other wrongdoing is a superfluous and often damaging requirement.

DETERMINING CUSTODY

The legal system over the years has been guided by three very different ideas on custody. The first notion, which strongly prevailed before the 1880's, sought to protect the father's best interests. It held that fathers should be awarded custody because children, through their labor, were important to maintaining the financial and economic interests of the family. These interests were identified with the father.

The second position, which began in the early 1900's, furthers the mother's best interests. It states that mothers generally should be awarded custody because they are the most important influence on infants and children, being naturally inclined to nurture and take care of their offspring. This position still is supported by many—perhaps most—lawyers and judges.

A third position has been introduced recently and slowly is gaining acceptance: It is the attempt to determine what is in the child's best interests. Neither male nor female is born with superior parenting skills. In some families mothers are more able and willing to assume primary responsibility for parenting, while in others the father clearly is the preferred choice. Of course, in some families the parents are equally able and willing. In contested cases a judge or jury ideally will examine relevant characteristics of both parents and will seek an arrangement that truly is in the child's best interest—one based on the parents'abilities and attitudes, not on their anatomy.

Custody issues in a recent case, for example, were resolved by awarding the house and its contents to the children. The parents, who wanted joint custody, alternately occupy the house. The father lives with the children in their home every other month and lives in an apartment in the same city during the intervening times while the children's mother lives with them.

In preparing for a custody decision, find out the lawyers' and judges' attitudes toward custody. If your lawyer's attitude seems to favor the best interests of the mother, get a different lawyer. If the attitudes of the opposing lawyer and presiding judge favor the best interests of the mother, your chances of gaining custody are more remote, though not completely lost. Winning custody will require strong evidence that the mother is not capable and that you are. Furthermore, if the attitudes in your community support the idea that custody should be determined in the best interests of the child, have the case heard by a jury. A jury may provide the most impartial review of all evidence.

What Evidence Is Important?

In awarding custody, judges also take into consideration the children's ages, sex, and number of brothers and sisters. Younger children and girls generally are awarded to mothers. A father's chances of gaining custody are increased if he has a son. Judges generally do not divide siblings. Brothers and sisters tend to be left together. In most courts, judges are interested in the children's views and preferences only after they are considered to be somewhat mature and rational—often about 12 to 14. Children much younger generally are not directly consulted by the judge, though their views may be made known by testimony supplied by psychologists, psychiatrists, and social workers employed by you, your wife, or the court.

Your Character and Resources

Provided you have the opportunity for an impartial hearing of all evidence, the judge (or jury) will be interested in information on how you and the childen's mother compare in terms of character and resources. Do you or the children's mother compare better in terms of:

- being trustworthy, reliable, and one in whom others have confidence
- actively attending a church or synagogue
- demonstrating stability in your vocation, interests, and activities
- not using alcohol and drugs
- having a job providing a sufficient and regular income
- managing money

Your Home Environment

Child-custody decisions also will include judgments on the ability of each parent to provide a quality home to the children. Information will include:

- the regularity of patterns for eating, schooling and homework, doing recreational activities together, performing household duties, and sleeping
- the moral character and reputation of your friends
- the quality of the schools and neighborhood
- the encouragement to develop extracurricular interests (music, sports, scouting)
- the availability of relatives and friends for the children
- the size of your home and quality of furnishings

Your Attitudes and Actions toward Children

Effective parenting does not emerge overnight. Effective parenting starts while children are infants and continues through the years. It embraces both the easy and difficult times. In deciding custody issues the judge will consider whether you or the mother compares more favorably in terms of:

- showing genuine love and concern toward your children
- taking an active interest in the children's physical, social, emotional, and academic development
- arranging regular and periodic visits to dentists and doctors
- attending children's performances
- meeting with teachers and attending school events
- imposing reasonable rules and regulations which protect their welfare
- shopping for their clothing
- encouraging their cultural development through after-school activities in music, art, and sports
- fostering church attendance and moral development
- insuring the children are properly dressed and bathed
- displaying an absence of abuse toward them

The most important yardstick to determine custody should be the welfare and best interests of the child. Although this is certainly the paramount factor the courts should consider, the prejudices discussed earlier often enter into the court's decisions. When a judge or jury is bound and determined that the mother should have custody, no matter what, the "best interests" test is often tossed aside. In determining the best interest of the children, prepare your case with the above characteristics in mind.

Recognize that the judge or jury will consider information on who has raised the children and the quality of that care. You will need to show that you have participated in the raising of your children and that you are able to run a household and care for their physical needs. Judges, of course, typically will assume that the woman runs the household and can care for the physical needs of the children. Thus, you must present strong evidence showing your involvement and its quality. This is best accomplished through witnesses who are mutual friends of both parties. A female testifying that the father can change diapers and feed the kids, for example, is especially effective. A father is hard-pressed to win the custody of his children, especially younger ones, if he is unable to prove this. He must show that he has made significant efforts in the proper raising of the children.

Temporary orders, as have been previously discussed, are also an important factor in a custody fight. If one can gain temporary custody and do a good job raising the children during the interim, this may be difficult for the the other party to overcome.

Acknowledging Children's Preferences

The children's preferences regarding living arrangements can be an important factor in determining custody, particularly with older children. Laws regarding children's participation vary greatly from state to state. In some states children have no rights or recourse to the courts while in others a court-appointed social worker or psychologist may represent them as their advocate. In some courts the judge will interview a child in chambers or allow him to testify in open court regarding his wishes; this usually happens when the child is 12 or older. Some states allow the child to decide with whom he wishes to live after reaching a certain age.

Whatever standards are used by judges and juries, the chance for a favorable ruling for fathers increases with advanced planning and proper actions. A review of the factors mentioned above and their application to your family situation before initiating action can be crucial to the success of the case. Your success may depend upon your ability to emphasize your strengths and to improve your weaknesses.

Visitation

Visitation rights for the noncustodial parent wishing to maintain contact with his children are very important. If at all possible, the noncustodial parent should avoid visitation rights which are nonspecific. He or she should make sure that the lawyer asks for visitation at definite times. Visitation "as agreed on by the parties," or "reasonable" visitation, may mean no visitation at all.

The frequency and duration of visitation is influenced by a number of factors. Age and sex of the children are often important considerations. The past record of a parent in visiting with the children along with the present desire to see them are also factors. The wishes of the custodial parent as well as the desires of the children are frequently considered. The physical problems of transportation and distance between the parents' home additionally may carry weight in determining the amount and frequency of visitation.

Child Support

Child support is a fact of life for the noncustodial parent. The courts customarily base the amount of support on the incomes of the parents along with their expenses and any special needs of the child. Each case is decided on an individual basis, and there is no set amount of child support for a child. Child support generally terminates either when the child reaches maturity or when the child's education is completed. Child support is not deductible by the noncustodial parent nor taxable to the custodial parent.

The amount set for the support of a child may be subject to change as discussed later. Because of the uncertain state of the economy and inflation, some child support awards may be tied to the rate of inflation, the consumer price index, or a similar indicator of the country's economic condition. That is, the support escalates (or falls) by the same percentage that a certain economic indicator does. This type of arrangement may preclude yearly court battles over raising of support.

Property

The laws regarding the division of property vary so widely from state to state that any attempt at a comprehensive discussion here would be impossible. However, an understanding of the two major theories of property—the common law rules of property, and the community property rule—will increase your general understanding of the basic issues. Because the laws within the 50 states differ, you need to consult a lawyer who is familiar with the specific state statutes governing property settlements in your state.

Under common law rules, the person who earns the income is the owner of the income and the property purchased by it. Regulations governing divorce typically provide for equalizing the division of property and continuing forms of support such as alimony. Under the community property rule, property acquired by husband and wife during the marriage is deemed to be jointly owned. Keep in mind that these rules may have little application to reality, especially when children are involved.

Debts, like property, must also be divided upon divorce. This division depends on factors such as the earning ability and financial position of both parties who incurred the debts, and, in the case of debts secured by property, who is awarded the property. Retirement pension plans, social security payments, and future income may also be considered by the court in the property division. Here again, it is necessary to consult an attorney in your state to ascertain the rules present in your jurisdiction.

When assessing your property assets, you must decide what constitutes a reasonable and equitable division of property. Having made this decision, attempt to have your wife agree to these terms around the bargaining table rather than in court. Your approach should be both reasonable and compromising. Anticipate that a court ordered division of property, though appropriate, is often unworkable and leaves neither side satisfied. Post-divorce problems often center on this dissatisfaction. Your lawyer can advise you on standards pertaining to the division of property in your jurisdiction and on the predilections of judges on this issue.

Alimony

Alimony has been the traditional common-law method of providing financial support for a woman after divorce. However, the Supreme Court has ruled that a state law which requires only husbands to pay alimony is unconstitutional, because it places the whole financial burden for the family on a divorced man. The Court refused to uphold the old notion that the man is primarily responsible for providing a home and its essentials, as the notion reflects a sexist attitude and is discriminatory. Increasingly, states are revising their alimony laws to allow men to claim alimony payments or to eliminate alimony.

The amount of alimony, like the amount of child support, is determined by a variety of factors. These include the wife's financial needs, her current job (if any) and work history, her future work prospects, the husband's financial situation and work prospects, and perhaps the degree of "fault" of each party in causing the divorce. Alimony is deductible by the husband and is taxed as part of the wife's income.

9

Keeping the Knots Untied

Living within the Law

Edwin Terry, Jr.

As a divorced father, accept the fact that legal issues will be your constant companion. The nature of your interactions with your children and former wife are likely to be governed more by the divorce decree and threats of future legal battles than by your good intentions. If, like most fathers, you have only "visitation privileges," accept the fact that the law allows for your children to eat with the neighbors and seek help for homework with friends while restricting their access to you.

The frustrations that arise out of any divorce, be it uncontested or a bitter custody fight, can place an unbearable strain on any divorced father. The father who loses the custody battle can expect various responses from his ex-wife. While some former spouses respond with understanding, others display uncooperative attitudes, extreme hostility, abrupt changes in visitation schedules, or interference in relationships with the children. Many fathers, following an uncontested divorce, are surprised to find the same range of responses from a former spouse. One effect of anger and animosity is to widen the differences and distance between the custodial and noncustodial parents. The noncustodial parent, feeling hurt and rejected, often wanders off seeking an escape from troubles. The gap then is further widened between the parents and between the children and the noncustodial parent. The same may happen when the mother "gives up" or "loses" custody to the father.

The reactions of the noncustodial parent can vary greatly. A father may withdraw from his children. Legal responsibilities may not be discharged. He may discontinue paying alimony and child support and see the children less and less. The loss is too great. The need to start "a new life," cutting all ties with the past, is an option some take. Often, however, the reaction is quite different. The father, thwarted in his attempts to establish a normal relationship with his children, reacts by either refusing to return the children after visitation periods or by spiriting them away to another city or state.

The court's response to these types of behavior is predictable. Unless the complaining father can show that consistent and irreparable harm has come to the children as a result of the mother's actions or neglect, the court invariably will protect the custodial parent, normalize the children's lives and punish the errant father. This protection is customarily achieved through issuing either a contempt of court or a *habeus corpus* action.

Being judged in contempt of court means that a party failed to abide by an order of the court. A typical situation occurs when the noncustodial parent refuses to return a child to the custodial parent, alleging that he is the better parent, that the child is not being cared for properly, or that the child desires to live with the noncustodial parent. This action, except in extraordinary circumstances, is strongly disfavored by the courts and rarely goes unpunished.

The court may punish a person held in contempt by a variety of methods. A jail sentence may be imposed on the offending party but is often suspended on the condition that the party abide by the court order. The court may also order the offender to pay a fine, or to pay the custodial parent's attorney's fees.

A *habeus corpus* action requires the person literally to "produce the body"—to bring the children to the court. Again, except in extreme circumstances, the granting of a writ of *habeus corpus* usually is automatic and swift. The initial intent of the judge is to return the children to their designated home and to encourage the development of consistency and regularity in their lives. The punishment following the return of children parallels that stemming from a contempt of court order.

While the divorce decree is a strong and mutually binding order, arrangements worked out jointly by you and your former wife, or hammered out by the decreee of a judge or jury, rarely remain constant. All families experience change. Occasional alterations in alimony, child support, and visitation schedules agreeable to both parties go unrecognized by the court. Remarriage, a move to another state, a severe illness, a significant financial change are but a few of the changes you can anticipate. Each major change may require you to reanalyze the divorce decree and to consider proposing alterations in it. You can avoid these and other future hindrances by three means: (1) work out an initial divorce decree that is generally acceptable to you, (2) learn to live within the law, or (3) go back to court to revise the decree. Any of these processes allows you to live a more rewarding and stress-free life.

CUSTODY AND VISITATION

Custody and visitation are a divorced father's only link to a normal relationship with his children. Therefore, utmost importance must be attached to setting up a viable, specific custody or visitation schedule at the time of divorce.

Do not assume that there will be no problems with custody or visitation. In fact, the opposite assumption is more likely true: There will be conflicts over custody or visitation. Thus, you will approach the issue with the intent to insure that the decree contains specific language detailing the arrangements. Vague provisions—such as "visitation as agreed upon by the parties," or "visitation at reasonable times and places"—are unworkable and essentially allow the custodial parent to dictate when, where, and for how long the noncustodial parent may be with the children. You are divorcing a partner with whom you cannot get along. While you hope for the best, you can expect your relationship to get worse following the divorce. Many fathers have learned painfully that their former wives never allow them to have regular and meaningful interactions with their children. Thus, strive for detail and specificity in the decree. Be sure it provides for regular and specific times for custody and visitation.

After discovering too late that you do not have "reasonable" visitation privileges, one solution is to return to court in an attempt to modify the original divorce decree. The difficulty of accomplishing this varies from state to state. Some judges will grant a modification if it is shown that both parties strongly support the change.

Fathers often want to change some specific provisions in the original divorce decree. For example, a father may want to decrease or increase the amount of time spent wtih his children. To effect this modification, a father generally must show the court an important life change—the child is older, the father is remarried, or one of the parents has moved to another locality—which justifies modifying the decree.

The noncustodial parents' refusal to return the child to the custodial parent is a problem being encountered with increasing frequency. This action invites retaliation by the custodial parent and the court and clearly demonstrates noncompliance with the law. It also jeopardizes any future attempts to prove that you are a good and qualified parent.

Should one parent refuse to return the child, at least three avenues are open to the custodial parent: self-help, *habeus corpus*, and contempt citations. Self-help, the most direct and expedient, can be fraught with difficulty and even danger. The custodial parent is obviously dealing with an emotionally charged situation which, as a rule, is best left to the police and legal systems. The remedy of *habeus corpus* is an effective means of regaining possession of the children. The court will return the children to the custodial parent unless unusual circumstances warrant a change. *Habeus corpus* can be particularly effective in interstate as well as intrastate disputes. The remedy of contempt of court is also available and involves the possibility of fining and/or jailing the disobedient parent.

Many fathers have found it necessary to ask courts to issue contempt citations when their former wives refused to allow them to see the children during the allotted visitation times or "at reasonable times and places." Courts will hold mothers in contempt when fathers are not allowed suitable visitation privileges. A lawyer often can press vigorously for proper sanctions by the court. Despite liberalizing mores and growing sexual equality, courts still are reluctant to place women in jail. Fathers should not withhold child support for a wife's failure to let him see the children. The courts correctly reason that, even when the mother's actions are unreasonable and in violation of a court order, the children still must be fed and housed. Some states are moving in the direction of tying visitation rights with child support, a move certainly welcomed by most fathers.

Child Support and Alimony

Child-support decisions are tied to many other issues. Most men recognize the need to continue providing financial support for their children and willingly contribute to their food, clothing, shelter, recreation, education, and medical and dental costs.

Monthly child support may be your largest single expense. It is paid from dollars already taxed, yet given to the children's mother who pays no taxes on it and generally can spend it whatever ways she sees fit. She need not justify how on whom the money is spent.

Some men see any financial payment—in addition to the property settlement—as an unjustifiable, constant, and irritating reminder of their former wives' holds over them. These feelings often produce hateful thoughts and spiteful actions which are both harmful and unproductive to men.

Many problems can be eliminated or at least lessened by taking proper precautions while preparing the divorce decree. The discussion which follows provides some guidelines.

Enforcement of support often occurs through a contempt of court proceeding. Many persons claim an inability to pay as the primary defense for nonpayment of support. While the court might have sympathy for a father who is denied visitation rights, most judges will not see this as a valid excuse for failure to pay support. Under the Uniform Reciprocal Support Act, one state may enforce another state's decree of child support, and may actually increase it if the circumstances warrant. The amount of child support or alimony specified in the divorce decree is not chiseled in stone. The court has the power to increase or decrease the amount of support paid when circumstances change. The granting of yearly increases in support is not uncommon in these days of high inflation. Other factors the court may take into account changes in income and marriage status, and increases in financial responsibilites including children born to either partner after the divorce. The court tends to be more reluctant to change the amount of alimony than the amount of child support.

A father generally cannot be sure the child support is being spent on the children. The courts have been reluctant to interfere with the custodial parent's discretionary spending of child-support money, fearing a flood of cases in this area.

The amount of child support typically is dependent upon the father's and mother's incomes, the amount of debts, the children's needs, and the life styles to which the family is accustomed. A customary method for determining child-support payments would be to decide how much it will take to continue meeting children's basic needs (that is, food, shelter, clothing, education, medical and dental expenses) and, when possible, meeting other desirable needs (private transportation and recreation). Child support traditionally is assumed by the father. For a mother to pay child support to the father is rare and newsworthy. Yet, courts increasingly are inclined to order a woman to pay child support if the man is awarded custody of the children, and her income is sizable. Courts also are beginning to enforce their orders with contempt of court citations for women who feel that, by virture of their sex, they are exempt from this obligation.

Persons paying child support should attempt to pay one set fee each month and not to be responsible for costs over which they have no control, for example, clothing and recreation. Avoid escalation clauses which increase support payments when your wages or the cost of living increases. If you assume responsibility for large costs, such as major medical, orthodontics, or private education, also retain authority to veto these expenses.

CUSTODY CAN BE CHANGED

Custody arrangements agreed to in the divorce decree rarely remain constant. All families can expect changes. The changes are slight for some. Minor changes may involve one parent's visiting with the children on Friday and Saturday rather than Saturday and Sunday, or their being together for the first 6 weeks of the summer rather than the last 6 weeks. However, other families will experience major changes. A move by one parent from the city or state inevitably leads to major custody rearrangements. The remarriage of one or both parents also tends to alter custody. These changes can significantly affect your relationship with your children.

Most changes in custody decided unilaterally by one parent or worked out jointly by both never come to the court's attention. Custody decisions can also be reviewed by the court and, if the evidence warrants, a formal change made in child custody.

How to Change Custody

In changing child custody you must reenter the legal arena. Seek the services of a competent lawyer, preferably one who has been successful in effecting changes in custody for clients. The lawyer first should help you review your evidence to determine your chances for changing custody.

Realize immediately that most courts are very reluctant to make custody changes. Judges want to minimize further disruptions in the lives of children and parents. Accordingly, the parent who has primary custody of children during the separation and divorce process is likely to be given primary custody following divorce. If you intend to be an active parent following your divorce, be as active as possible prior to and during the divorce. If possible, try to get primary custody of the children during the separation period.

Judges also recognize that strong hatred and jealousies between the former spouses can cause them to lash out at one another. Alimony and child custody often are the two remaining threads of the former relationship, and both parents may attempt to manipulate and alter these. The court's reluctance to change custody additionally stems from its belief that prior agreements should be honored and that a new one is no more likely to be honored. Strong and conclusive evidence is needed to alter custody arrangements.

In order for fathers to change custody, evidence must strongly show that the mother is unfit and that the child's best interests are not being served. Furthermore, evidence must strongly show that the father is suitably fit and that he can provide a home which serves the child's best interests.

The following characteristics help to define suitable parents. Evidence gathered on these points has been used to justify changes in custody. Remember that the descriptions apply equally to mother or father, and that either parent can seek changes in custody. Child care and neglect are judged on the following conditions:

- not arriving home promptly after work
- frequently being away from home at night
- alcohol or drug abuse
- incest or other socially unacceptable forms of sexual conduct
- conviction of a criminal offense by parent or child
- conflicts and problems with stepchildren or stepparents
- remarriage to a person of a different race or lower social and economic status
- the parent having a number of extramarital affairs or living with another out of wedlock
- changes in the parent's physical or mental conditions
- impeding the ability of the other parent to maintain strong and wholesome relationships with the children (e.g., denial of visitation rights)
- negative statements one parent makes about the other
- irregular preparation of nutritious meals
- lack of cleanliness of home, clothes, and children
- many children per room in home
- failure to provide a suitable place and time for children to study
- inattention to children's educational development and school conduct

- termination of, or change in, religious training
- failure to recognize and attend to academic, social, and emotional problems in children generally detected by teachers, neighbors, and other knowledgeable adults
- noninvolvement in children's hobbies and school activities
- little time spent between parent and child
- few phone calls, letters, and other forms of interest displayed toward children when not in custody
- inattention to children's health needs
- providing unsuitable child care while away from home
- financial irresponsibility
- frequent or abrupt moves

In a petition to change custody, the judge will be interested in the information you bring to the court. But your case is strengthened by having principals, teachers, psychologists, social workers, ministers, and other professional persons testify on your behalf. As they presumably are more objective and will consider the child's best interest above those of either parent, their testimony may carry greater authority. Testimony by friends and neighbors, while less objective, can also be extremely beneficial. Don't overlook any source of information which may show that your former spouse's conduct is unsuitable and that yours is suitable.

Child-custody changes require two forms of evidence—one demonstrating the unfitness of your former spouse and the other demonstrating your fitness. It is not enough for you to show how unfit the children's mother is. Unless you show your behavior to be much better than hers, the judge may make the child a ward of the court because he sees you, too, as unfit. To gain custody, you must show your behavior to be exemplary. Return to the lists presented above and on pages 168–172, and examine your own conduct in these terms. If you compare favorably to the children's mother on a number of characteristics, your chances of gaining custody are significantly improved.

10

Managing Your Household

Jane Manaster

Until now, there always was someone to back you up—even to blame—when things went wrong. Well, those days are gone. Now, you are wholly responsible for the running of your home. When you run out of toilet paper, find tomato soup dripping down the back of the refrigerator, see the parakeet dead at the bottom of its cage, or realize that half a bottle of aspirin is unaccounted for it is your responsibility.

On the other hand, if you want fish sticks five nights in a row, or football instead of sitcoms on TV, jungle-print bedsheets, or an unshared razor, you have one less person to contend with.

Running a home is an enormous responsibility. The best way to cope is to pare down the chores you were taught to consider essential so that your home becomes plain and habitable rather than a show piece or a pig pen.

There are two keys to running your home: your information and your attitudes. If you try and model your home after those that appear on television, you strive for fairyland. If you try to model your home based on what you read, you will panic at the countless jobs you feel expected to undertake. When my first child developed a rash, my cousin—also a new mother—warned me, "Don't read Dr. Spock. He'll make you imagine dozens of terrible possibilities, and chances are the spots will have gone by morning." More succinctly, get good advice from people who you respect and who have been through this before. Also, use your own judgment. Organize your home the way you think it should be organized. You will probably find the few basics you need to know revolve on common sense and attitude you muscle up yourself.

Instead of adding to your burden by worrying how your children will adjust, concentrate on your own adjustment. Their days will still begin with crawling out of bed, finding socks that match, hurriedly eating breakfast, locating the right homework, and going off to school.

FOODS

As you think about moving into your new apartment or home, you realize that there are a few duties that have to be tackled. You must buy and fix food, which requires some understanding of marketing, storing, and cooking. You must keep the home clean enough to ward off health-department visitors, and safe from fire, poisoning, and other ghastly hazards. You must make sure that young children are not alone at home, but cared for at all times. You must not neglect medical problems, check-ups, and immunizations. You will find you can live more comfortably if you have good relationships with the school authorities, your relatives, and neighbors.

Let's tackle the issue of food first. By feeding everyone halfway decently, the household will be off to a head start. Your children probably know a lot more about nutrition that you do. Nutrition, currently, is a popular area in social studies. There are four main food groups: milk, meat, fruit and vegetables, bread and cereal. One needs to draw several portions from each group every day. By doing so fairly religiously, there is no need to pop supplementary vitamin pills. Vitamins are nutrients found in various foods in their natural state. They are also commercially added to some foods, such as milk and bread, to ensure that children get all they need.

The size of the servings of each food depends upon the size of the consumer. As a rule, children rarely undereat. Moreover, don't judge your worth as a father by the amount of food your children consume. By examining the different food groups more closely, you can see your choices at a glance.

Milk Group

This includes milk, cheese, cottage cheese, yogurt, and ice cream. Milk provides calcium, high-quality protein, and vitamin A, as well as other good things to a lesser degree. Children under 9 need from 2 cups to 2 pints—depending upon who is doing the talking and who you believe. Children 9-12 need 3 cups, and teenagers 4 cups. A 1-inch cube of Cheddar is equivalent to half a cup of milk, a half cup of ice cream is equal to a fourth cup of milk, and so on.

Meat Group

The meat group supplies top-grade protein for body tissues to be built or repaired, and also contains valuable minerals, the best known being iron. Aim for two daily sevings (2 to 3 ounces) of meat, fish, poultry, or eggs (which are counted as a half serving each). Peanut butter and soybeans also are proteins.

Fruits and Vegetables Group

Try to provide four servings a day. Include one that is high in vitamin C (such as a citrus fruit) and one high in vitamin A (maybe a green-leaf vegetable or carrots). Fruit and vegetables are so obviously good that it is hard to accept that they need to be subdivided to make up diet patterns.

Bread and Cereal Group

Again, four daily servings are needed. A half cup of cooked cereal, a slice of bread, or a bowl of cold cereal equals one serving. Check labels to be sure the contents are whole grain, enriched, or restored. Thus, whether you have holier-than-thou children who eat only nubbly brown bread or regular children who eat the soft, white variety, they still are being nourished if the label has the magic words.

Going through this rigmarole satisfies the conscience but not the appetite unless you translate it into meals. Here, again, you can get yourself overinvolved, so break down a week's meals into something both manageable and palatable.

Breakfast

You don't have to prepare all breakfasts to feel like the world's finest father. Teach children how to fix eggs without setting themselves ablaze. Cub Scouts must cook in order to attain their Wolf status. If the Boy Scouts of America think cooking breakfast is safe at 8 years old, you should go along with that. A single scrambled egg, or the 3 minute boiled variety, is speedy and satisfying. Nothing is easier than preparing cold cereal. Cereals are quick and often nutritious. Frozen waffles and pancakes with syrup may not hold off the hunger pangs until lunchtime, so supplement these meals with fruit or a mid-morning snack, be sure they get protein, cereal, or cheese on toast. Milk is essential. Orange, grapefruit, or tomato juice (the latter two not usually popular with children), or half an orange or grapefruit, balance the meal but can be digested just as easily later in the day if you are in a rush.

Lunch

Take full advantage of school lunches. They can be moderately priced, varied, and convenient (a factor important to maintaining your sanity). Some children find school lunches disgusting. However well a nutritionist has planned them, lunches not eaten do no good. Talk with the children about their lunches. If they eat only the bread roll, they are better off choosing one or two of their favorites each week for a treat (the pizza and the baked chicken) and taking sack lunches the other days.

In preparing sack lunches, don't go crazy making every day a fiesta; yet don't be cruel by expecting them to be overjoyed with the same old stuff each day. Many children prefer peanut butter and jelly to anything exotic you may offer, so don't willfully spoil the brief noontime period of pleasure that comes daily between math and spelling.

If, however, your children are open to variety, try cheese, tuna, (unless the building is overheated, and you fear bacterial infection), bologna (until the day they tell you it is made out of rats' tails), or peanut butter with honey. As an alternative to sandwiches, send along crackers or celery with cream cheese or peanut butter, a hard-cooked egg with a packet of salt taken from a hamburger place, or a leftover hamburger or hot dog. Add a piece of fruit, but not one that is too big, or hard to peel. Include something like a handful of grapes, an unspotted banana, peach, plum, pear, or a tangerine. Also, send along pretzels, potato or corn chips. Buy chips that say "No Preservatives" since they taste much better, and buy big sacks to be put in plastic sandwich bags. The tiny packages cost too much money. Lastly, wrap a couple of cookies or a slice of cake in plastic. The food items they do not like they can trade to other children, or, sin of sins, sell and buy dessert from the cafeteria.

Dinner

This meal often causes the biggest worries for fathers. Rushing home from work, greeting the children, and wondering what there is to eat is a common plight. Before considering dinner menus, remember that a night out once in a while is a good idea. Enroll your children in every franchise birthday club, and the gift coupons will ease the guilt about buying fried chicken and midwinter ice cream.

Besides meals, snacks play a part in the day's eating pattern and in the budget. No child has been known to stop eating a packet of chips or cookies before the last one is crunched. Your children are unlikely to be different, so only allow a certain amount to be available. If you make a weekly visit to the supermarket, hide anything likely to be eaten before its time. Also, establish the rule that no packet, jar, or can can be opened or finished by a child without permission. This way you may find the remaining pickle or slice of processed cheese annoying, but at least it's a reminder to buy more.

Though many divorced fathers have years of experience in the kitchen and the home, others have virtually none and do not know where to start. You soon will ask yourself some of these questions. How long can meat sit in the refrigerator before it turns green? How many days does a loaf of bread last? If I forget to take the unsightly bits out of the chicken before baking it, will we be poisoned? The answers to some questions are obvious, but there are ground rules. Refrigerate or freeze all meat. Frozen meats last virtually forever. Refrigerated meats should be prepared within 3 to 4 days. Once cooked, meat is safe refrigerated for a few days longer. For example, you can chop and fry an onion in a couple of tablespoons of fat over fairly low heat, then add 2 pounds of ground beef. Cook it, with an occasional stir, until the meat is brown instead of red; then, once cooked, you can refrigerate the meat for future use. One pound of ground beef will make a comfortable meal for four if used for cottage pie, meatballs (add a handful of breadcrumbs), spaghetti sauce, meat loaf, or other simple favorites.

Cake mixes, when first introduced, were not popular with women because they judged the quality of their meals by their labor and hardship. Ready mixes were seen as too easy to be good.

Some fathers may have the same unnecessary hangups. Don't judge the quality of meals by the amount of time you spend preparing them. You soon will learn that a 15-minute prepared dinner consisting of milk, a salad, Ragu spaghetti, bread, and canned fruit may be more popular and nutritious than a more costly dinner slavishly prepared.

Most fathers will want to simplify and economize. The two can go together with proper planning. Begin by preparing a menu for at least 2 weeks. Consult the school menu at the same time. Preparing a menu allows you to plan a balanced menu, to alternate the foods prepared at home with those available at school, and to shop more wisely. This also allows you to make fewer decisions—that in itself is a godsend.

Combine frozen and prepared dinners with those which require some preparation on your part. Frozen fish, chicken, and meat pies are popular and economical. Frozen TV dinners are more complete meals and also quick, but are a bit more expensive. Keep these for emergencies. Buy a slow cooker in which to prepare soups, stews, meats, and casseroles. The food goes in before you leave for work and is ready when you come home.

Also, always try to prepare enough food to have at a second meal. For example, a 2-pound meat loaf can last through two to three dinners.

A 4-pound chicken, baked or roasted, can be eaten hot once, then in salad or sandwiches, or over rice mixed with a can of mushroom soup. Or that same chicken could be combined with various vegetables, a 16-ounce can of V-8 and some water (plus salt and pepper) to prepare a delicious chicken soup for two dinners.

Simplify aand Economize

Remember, strive for simplicity and economy. Elegant and expensive meals will not provide the rewards you expect.

A shelf of cookbooks is intimidating, but a couple of fast-selling paperbacks are reassuring. I recommend Peg Bracken's *I Hate to Cook Book* and *Better Homes and Gardens New Cook Book*. Recipes on labels and boxes usually are excellent. They presume barely any experience and no exotic ingredients.

Some fast meals are too simple to have written recipes, and are tremendously successful: A can of chunky chicken soup heated and poured over a can of chow mein noodles: canned macaroni and cheese layered with tuna and browned under the broiler: hot dogs cut up and heated with a hearty shake of Worcestershire sauce, ketchup, mustard, and curry powder served on packaged mashed potatoes with a huge glass of ice water—inventiveness and spunky kids make a varied diet possible and enjoyable.

On the days when you see 6-feet-tall teenagers apparently thriving on candy bars and French fries, you may be tempted to give up your good intentions, but don't. Teeth, skin, mental alertness, and physical vigor can fall apart abruptly without sound nourishment.

Many children fuss about vegetables served plain, but will readily eat them in salads or soup. Keep your supply of sweetened and starchy snack food to a minimum as children have an inherent ability to find and devour them. Children almost invariably eat much more sugar than is good for them.

Don't be hoodwinked into spending a lot on foods labeled "organically grown," "natural," or "health food." The cost is always higher than the regular fare. A recent car trip through Southern California raised my scepticism when the drive was enlivened by signs urging, "Organically grown fruit 18 miles," and "Stop! Organically grown apricots and peaches 5 miles." The signs were barely visible through the smog.

If you are setting up a home from scratch or are replenishing one, keep the following foods in store so that both the ingredients and full meals are always available. The list goes beyond your simple survival needs and bridges the difference between your life as a makeshift existence and your having a resourceful home.

Basic Foods To Buy:

LIST 1

salt
pepper
vanilla
cinnamon
bay leaves
oregano
Worcestershire sauce
soy sauce
ketchup (cheaper in large
    bottles)
mustard
coffee
tea bags
sugar (5-pound bag)
powdered sugar (1 pound)
flour (5-pound bag)
pancake mix
syrup
Peanut butter (name brands
    more expensive but gen-
    erally better tasting than
    store brands)
cheap jelly to go with
    peanut butter
better jelly, preserves or honey

cold breakfast cereal,
   eg, corn flakes
hot breakfast cereal,
   eg, oatmeal
salad oil
shortening (2 pounds)
cider vinegar
sandwich spread
salad dressing
some of the following:
   baked beans
   spaghetti in tomato sauce
   Ranch-style beans
   chili with or without beans
   corned beef hash
   Vienna sausages
popcorn
rice
spaghetti and noodles
cocoa powder
dried milk powder
canned fruit
cake mix
soup, canned or in packages
Jello, packaged milk desserts
   and gelatin pudding
canned tomatoes, tomato
   sauce, tomato paste
canned vegetables (avoid
   hominy, beets, and lima
   beans unless some of you
   like them.)
baking powder
macaroni and cheese dinner
Ragu spaghetti sauce
soaps for bathing,
   dishwasher, and laundry
   (and bleach)
sandwich bags (plastic and

  paper)
aluminum foil
plastic wrap
napkins

These items are to stay in the refrigerator:

biscuits
butter or margarine
milk
cheese
eggs
mayonnaise

  The following list gives you some ideas for what you may consume in a week. Of course, the range of foods available is so extensive that you can easily come up with a wholly different list.

LIST 2

  For a household of one adult and two to three pre-teenage children, this list should provide ample food for a week when used in conjunction with items already on the shelf (such as ketchup, sugar, and coffee).

1 dozen eggs
2-2½ gallons milk
1 pound margarine
three-four loaves sandwich
    bread
hot dog or hamburger buns
two packets cookies, or one
    packet and one box cake
    mix
large packet chips or large
    sack of pretzels
8-10 pounds potatoes
1 pound rice
3½ to 4-pound chicken

six pork chops
packet of hot dogs
1-1½ pounds cheese
two of the following: broccoli,
    spinach, squash, green
    beans
two-10 ounce packets of corn
    or peas
two heads of lettuce and
    tomatoes and celery for
    salad
three cans or packets of soup,
    the fixings for homemade
    soup
one can tomatoes and tomato
    paste
1 pound bacon
one dessert pie
½ gallon icecream
three 6-ounce cans frozen
    orange juice, or one
    46-ounce can

In addition to foods, kitchens need a selection of utensils and appliances. If you have the fundamentals, the following list will allow you to fill in the gaps so that you can whip up anything from a milk shake to a banquet.

LIST 3

A 9-inch and a 6-inch skillet
    (Cast iron skillets are the
    best.)
One 4-quart pan with lid
One 6-quart pan with lid
One 8-quart pan with lid
    loaf pan (preferably,
    aluminum with Teflon)
one 2-quart casserole

one 4-quart casserole
13x9 inch baking dish for
  sheet cakes, turkey, and
  anything in between
cookie sheet (Buy good
  quality.)
measuring cups
plastic measuring jug
can opener
small and large knives for
  cutting
mixing bowls
strainer
grater, potato peeler, wooden
  spoon, gadgets you enjoy

Besides these, and your regular dishes and silverware, you may want a few small electrical appliance. These invariably are more attractive and functional in other peoples' lives than when cluttering your kitchen, so don't assume they are all essential. The following, however, will be welcome:

toaster (Much quicker and safer, and more energy efficient than using the oven broiler. If there are only two of you, a small broiler oven is handy and can function like a toaster.)

blender (Terrific for milk shakes, daiquiris, nutritious 30-second breakfasts and snacks made from yogurt, oatmeal, wheatgerm, fruit, and honey. Children can learn to use them safely.)

bag sealer (When you make a stew, spaghetti, or in fact anything in greater quantity than needed for one meal, this appliance will heat seal the leftovers in heavy gauge plastic sacks. The sacks can be frozen, and later thawed in a pan of hot water in a matter of minutes.)

microwave oven (Luxuries soon become necessities. This is true for microwave ovens which prepare food quickly. Original preparation time is cut in half or more. Reheating occurs in seconds to a few minutes.)

slow cookers (Some people call these by one brand name—Crock pots. As previously explained, food put in the slow cooker by 8 a.m. is ready by dinner time. The cooking is safe and economical.)

iron and ironing board (While no-iron clothes prevail, you will find the need for the occasional use of an iron and a collapsible ironing board.)

In case you have a virgin kitchen, hunt for the following:

some dish rags to wash and dry dishes

regular old rags to mop up the floor

detergent (like Comet)

plastic pan scrubs to use on your so-called non-stick pans

old coffee cans or plastic containers to put everything from flour to to left over spinach in

paper towels (if you believe in throwing money away)

Finally, before leaving this part of the home, here are some of the more common dangers you can avoid:

Keep bleach and ammonia well away from each other.

Have anything poisonous or caustic *well out of reach.*

Don't put dangerous items in innocuously marked containers, like empty peanut butter jars.

Tape a list of poisons and their antidotes or treatments on the door of the refrigerator.

Don't let anyone stick a hand down the waste disposal.

Make little hands choose little knives.

Tie back long hair that could cause tragedies if caught in an appliance or the waste disposal.

Keep clothes and other items that burn well away from the stove top.

Life Beyond the Kitchen

Food plays an important part in your life, but be sure everyone stays healthy to enjoy it. Take your children to a pediatrician or general practitioner and to the dentist for an annual checkup. Birthday week is a good time to do this since the birthday serves as a reminder, and the children will look forward to learning how much they have grown and gained.

Schools are very particular about immunizations, and you should be, too. Fearsome epidemics occur because parents are remiss. Have your children see shots as a privilege rather than a cruelty, and recognize how lucky they are that you are helping them avoid gruesome diseases. Don't put off required school or camp checkups until the last moment as it may be impossible to get an appointment.

Besides the annual checkups, see or, at least, speak to the children's doctor whenever you have a question. Doctors go through medical school to become expert at diagnosing and treating sickness—not as an easy route to becoming a millionaire. It is unfair to call them at 3 a.m. if your child has been vomiting for the past 15 hours just because your nervousness has turned to panic. Likewise, it is unfair to call Thursday when the child has been running a fever since Monday. Don't feel like a jerk calling. You are responsible for seeing what the matter is. Doctors won't thank you for undertaking their job until the point at which you decide you need advice.

Young children run into all sorts of fairly minor sicknesses that make them very ill usually for a short time. Preschoolers get alarming fevers with ear infections. They can go to bed a bit tireder than normally and be burning up by the middle of the night, or crying for hours with an earache. Let the doctor check it out and treat the infection. Be obedient about keeping the child home.

Coughs, intestinal upsets, stomach flu, chest and head colds, even pneumonia—there are plenty of troubles which can hit your children. For the most part sicknesses hit during the winter months, but swimmer's ear hits in the summer when you feel everyone should be well.

Don't get mad and send your children off to school when they are not well. Instead, be especially compassionate and loving. Call into work and explain you won't be there. Don't leave sick young children alone in the house, nor have an older child take the day off school to help you out unless it is honestly imperative.

If the child is sick enough to sleep all day, don't wake him or her up because you think you will be kept busy all night. The sleep is not a substitute for night sleep, but a way of overcoming the sickness.

After the sleeping stage, which usually ends when the fever breaks, allow the child as much television as wanted. This is a satisfactory way of keeping the child quiet and still. When the attraction wanes, far sooner than you would have dreamed, be ready with felt-tip pens, scissors, old magazines and newspapers that can be colored and cut up, simple untaxing books and comics, or a stack of children's magazines often available from garage sales. Also, have a pack of cards handy, and take time to play the kind of games you used to enjoy yourself. Children upwards of four can play "Beat Your Neighbor": divide the pack into two, face down. Alternate turning up a card, each "paying" four cards for an ace, three for a king, two for a queen and one for a jack. The winner is the one to end up with the whole pack. Another good game is Concentration, which some call "Spread." All the cards are laid randomly face down on the floor, and you alternate turning up two, trying to match a pair, turning them down if you fail, taking another try if you succeed. The winner has the most pairs when all the cards have been matched.

In sickness or in health, be extremely careful with medicine. Keep it beyond reach, and avoid possible accidents. Chocolate-flavored laxative pills are no less tempting than orange-flavored children's aspirin. These latter come in bottles of 36, which is supposedly not a lethal dose. But why take risks? Adult aspirin tastes horrible but can kill if taken in quantity. If aspirin is needed (and they often are very effective), and your child is a bad swallower, give the tablets with a spoonful of jelly washed down with a glass of water. Most doctors suggest a child with an upset stomach should stop eating rather than rely on medicine.

The following are the basics for a medicine cabinet:

aspirin
laxative
antidiarrheal
first-aid spray
Anti-histamine (if your area exudes allergy problems)
cough syryp
bandaids
thermometer
antibiotic cream
peroxide and witch hazel (optional)
toothbrushes and toothpaste

Your home must be cleaned periodically, but you are unlikely to find someone like the "Brady Bunch's" Alice scrubbing and polishing all the time. This part of your domestic life needs careful attention to begin wth. After the first few weeks of trial and error, establish a routine which allows you to get the job done while still ignoring it most of the time. Don't make beds. Train children to clean up their floors once a week. The home looks a whole lot more welcoming when tidy, and probably children feel more comfortable bringing friends in if it doesn't look like the aftermath of a tornado. But your family can decide that together. If the shared part of the home is presentable, everyone should be free to choose how their own territory looks, within reason.

Bathrooms do not need a top-to-bottom cleaning every day, though it is revolting when the sink looks like birds roosted above it because of the toothpaste spat left. Have a toilet brush, cloth, and a canister of Comet under the sink, and clean the toilets every week. Under the rim of the actual bowl tends to get disgusting.

A cleaning woman every two weeks is a wonderful extravagance, and unless you are really strapped for money worth every cent. Check with friends (many share the maid's day fifty-fifty) or consult the Yellow Pages for maid services. Compare prices before making your decision. Some charge a lot extra for bringing their own cleaning equipment, and if you are well stocked already you don't need theirs. If someone on the block or in your building has a "treasure," take advantage. Figure out which chores you hate most and pay to have these done. The washing, for instance, is a breeze, and the children are not averse to helping with this. Giving the kitchen and bathroom a good cleaning though, is something you'd likely prefer to have done for you. If you have a pre-schooler, you may find an arrangement with a young parent who is willing to bring his or her own child and combine cleaning with sitting.

Washing clothes is easy enough whether you have your own machine or traipse to the laundromat. Have enough clothes at one time so that you only have to do it once a week. Keep the children smelling wholesome, but don't let them get away with throwing everything in the dirty clothes' holder rather than hanging things up. Jeans can last several days without a wash. Shirts, shorts, and socks can't. Make sure each child has about 10 of each so that the weeks when you fall behind they are not fretting through a smelly mass of discarded clothes to get themselves off to school. If you are unlucky enough to have coats or heavy sweaters that will not survive a washing machine (and if they do not bear the dreaded label "Professionally Dry Clean Only") you can throw them in the laundromat's dry cleaning machine where you pay by the pound.

Dirty curtains and small kitchen and bathroom mats need attention fairly frequently. Watch for dirt rather than setting a mandatory date for washing them. Bed linens need changing every couple of weeks if your children bathe fairly regularly. If they don't, or if you live in a warm part of the country and have no air conditioning, once a week is preferable.

While clothes need only occasional mending nowadays, have light and dark thread and a couple of needles around. Learn how to sew on buttons, mend small tears, and hem. Teach the children too, as it costs a lot of money to have someone do these minor jobs for you. Too-long jeans can be shortened easily with heat tape but more fragile fabric cannot. If you are really helpless with a needle and thread, and more proficient with faucet fixing and electrical repairs, hunt for a neighbor who will trade off chores with you.

Caring for Children When Away

As a parent you are on call 24 hours a day. You must make provisions for the children for when you are not at home and in case of emergencies. Several states have laws which forbid children being left alone at night under a certain age. Remember, your child has already gone through the shock of losing a full-time parent. You must see they are well cared for when you are away. This also allows you to relax more. Some schools provide supervised care when classes are over, or churches and other special centers enable you to finish your working day without worrying about the children going back to an empty home. After-school care should be top priority. If you live within reach of a college or university, you have a good chance of finding a student whose schedule and financial situation make a good bet for exchanging sitter service for pocket money, dinner, and the joy of being with children. If your home is large enough, consider providing room and board in exchange for child care and domestic duties. Lay down rules for both the children and sitters about where and what they can do.

Day care for the preschoolers varies tremendously in cost and quality. A woman taking care of half a dozen children in her own home is probably preferable for most youngsters rather than a nursery school of 20 children which vows to have them reading at three and a half. Don't be tempted when care centers purport to be "challenging." Everything is challenging to a little kid. Get references and suggestions from the principal or secretary at the school your older children attend, other parents, people you work with. Check out their suggestions carefully yourself, and if anything about them displeases you, say "No." You have enough to worry about without being anxious about a little one running out into the street or being stuck in a crib 6 hours a day. A college degree in early child care is not necessarily an adequate substitute for tender loving care. Don't feel jealous if your children love their sitter, day care center, or after-school care. Share their pleasure and enjoy hearing about their day.

Unless you are lucky enough to live within a few blocks of the school, you will need to make arrangements about transportation.

Where there are no buses, car pooling can often be arranged to suit everyone. You may prefer to drive mornings rather than afternoons, one week in four, rather than Mondays and alternate Wednesdays. You may drive in exchange for parking your child at the other parents' home, or pay toward a neighbor's gas bill. Whatever you choose, arrange it all carefully. Don't rely on a haphazard scheme which leaves everyone in a mess. All the small stabilities in your children's lives add up to their general feelings of security.

Visit your school about three times yearly (October, February, and May are good). Many schools encourage parents to speak with the teacher, eat in the lunchroom a couple of times a semester, take part in special projects, and attend the concerts. Do as much as you can. Join the PTA and understand just what is going on. To have a parent present like everyone else means a lot to children. If, however, you are not wanted at a particular event or in the lunch room, don't push. Respect your children's requests however awkwardly expressed.

As the children grow older, they are bound to become more involved in extracurricular activities. Some of these cost money, all of them cost time, and most are likely to involve you. Be prepared for these times.

Though budgeting is a separate issue, it has to be somewhat considered here. You will need to decide how to use your most easily expendable commodities: time and money. You have neither the time nor money to meet all requests made of you. You will need to meet basic needs you and your children have. Any extra time and money can be used on those things which are important but not crucial. For example, decide whether you can be involved in the children's classes and activities.

Young children have needs beyond home and school. Involvement in music, art, scouting, and sports are desirable. In considering these activities, remember that in many instances you get what you pay for. For example, group piano lessons at a community school probably will not advance your child's skill as speedily as private (more expensive) lessons. However, one teacher may fire up a whole group and have them learning enthusiastically while another will be instantly disliked and achieve nothing. Similarly in sport. There are superb pros working with city recreation departments and less competent ones teaching at the posh club where you center your own social life.

When you are making the choice of extracurricular activities, listen to your children's request. If you insist on them taking poetry reading while they prefer pottery, anticipate all sorts of unpleasant resistance. If you think your shrimp would be toughened up by football, and he believes karate would work better, he has the edge over you. School is mandatory 6 hours a day. When it comes to planning leisure time, children need as much freedom of choice as you do.

There are far more things for your children to do than you realize. Hear out their requests; yet, make the decisions so that you don't spend all your waking hours driving, watching, refereeing or feeding. Recognize your limitations. Don't be blackmailed into choosing the socially preferred ballet school if there is an equally good one close at hand. Don't be cajoled into buying an expensive musical instrument because your child has a hero who plays one. Tell the children your limitations. They will understand.

Some of the activities currently popular with boys and girls are soccer, disco dancing, cooking, guitar, crafts, art, gymnastics, camping skills, tumbling, karate, and *kung fu.*

Be insistent about practicing and attending classes, but if it becomes a continual hassle, you are better off allowing the child to drop out at the end of the course or semester rather than building up antagonism. By keeping your investments low, the cost of giving up an activity is minimal. Remember; we all develop and then lose interest in people, activities, and ideas. Do not put a child down because photography or basketball did not work out. Some parents keep children in an unwanted activity because of its ease and convenience to them.

Weekends are important to both you and the children. Though family councils and democratic gatherings work better on television than in real life, sit down and figure out the best schedule with respect for each other. Bedtime will have to be more flexible, and children can learn very quickly that you like to sleep late on Saturday rather than watch cartoons at 6:30. Help them out, though. Leave a package of cereal out, buy milk in small enough containers for the youngest child to be able to lift and pour. Be firm about the television volume being kept low and no one, especially overnight guests, talking above a whisper until you surface.

With the best will in the world, it is hard to organize weekends. Don't push anyone into doing anything unwanted on Saturday mornings as it sours the whole weekend. If you enjoy going out Friday or Saturday evenings, find a teenager who will contract with you to sit on a regular basis. Forfeit a couple of dollars to the sitter the weeks you choose to stay home. Make sure, though, that the sitter reciprocates your consideration, and agrees to provide a substitute of whom you approve if something prevents his or her coming. Most teenagers are out of sitting and into dating by 15-16 years old, so don't think an ideal arrangement will last forever. Boys also make great baby-sitters for your sons and daughters, and many enjoy the unusual opportunity to make money without having to mow lawns or prove their muscular strength. Be sure to leave sitters a phone number where you or a chosen adult can be reached, the doctor's number, and a set of rules to be observed—bedtime, what can be eaten, telephone use, whether a friend may come over, how much time should be spent entertaining your children, who gets to choose TV programs, which of your belongings (like the stereo or hair dryer) can be used.

Pay baby-sitters a minimum of 2 hours, even if you plan to be gone just for one and let them arrange how to split the money. Unless you are out swinging every evening, never feel the least bit guilty about leaving your children with a sitter. Your children may secretly wish to have someone else care for them for awhile. Agreeable teenagers are a lot more fun to have around in the evening than you are after a full day's work and parenting.

Besides day-to-day events, there are special occasions to be considered. Most of us have an extended family—relatives outside of our immediate household. In addition to staying on friendly terms with them and rotating the entertaining at Thanksgiving, Christmas, and the like, consider their offers of assistance. Grandparents who offer to stay with you for a week and give you a break, or have your children to their home, should be thanked rather than turned down. When with them, avoid any subversive talk against you or your ex-wife.

Birthdays are much more important to children than to adults. They are a splendid occasion for your children to be both aware and proud of their home, family, and friends. Have a party on the actual day, or as close to it as practical. Ignore the current trend to take the children roller skating or to a hamburger place, and instead put on a special bash. Don't be intimidated or perturbed at the thought of a bunch of youngsters tearing your place apart. They are likely to be sufficiently used to adult authority to listen to you. Decide on the time and money you intend to spend, and then discuss with the celebrant how to organize it. Younger children love to compete, whether in a three-legged running race or in pencil and paper games. Schools tend to frown on individual excellence in the primary grades, and this gives them a chance to show off. Vary the games so that the brainy, the quiet, the inventive, and the athletic children all get a fair chance at the half dozen prizes you award. You will find it quite easy to choose the winners.

Here are a few games that are easy to set up and lots of fun:

Outdoors. Buy a large sack of marbles or plastic cowboys and Indians. Hide them all over the place...finders/keepers.

Line all the children up according to size. Have them alternately take one step forward or back to form two teams for soccer, Red Rover, and volleyball.

Choose the slowest child to play Grandmother in "Grandmother's Footsteps"—the game in which everyone creeps up stealthily, and the Grandmother glances over her shoulder and sends whoever is moving back to base.

Inside. Several times over, hide a button for them to find.

Set 10-20 objects on a tray, let them look for 30 seconds, then cover the tray and see who can remember the most.

Wrap a small gift in at least a dozen layers of paper; have the children sit in a circle, unwrapping a layer each time you lift the needle off the record. Children who lose at every other game can win this.

Have everyone jump up and down, taking the needle from the record every few seconds. Last to sit down is out, until all but one are gone.

Hide and go seek can be played for hours, but set danger spots off limits.

Feed the children junk food—sugar-laden punch, ice cream, cake with plastic frosting. This is all part of living.

Summer, with weeks of empty days to be filled, is a different story. Check all the local resources: The city recreation department, YMCA, YWCA, Scouts, churches, and private camps all offer summer programs. Choose the one that best fits your children's interests and your budget. Often the city-run ones are the best, providing for lots of children whose interests and experience vary in sophistication. Privately-run camps have the advantage of including transportation. Include some physical activity (swimming, hiking daily). A daily dose of pioneer crafts or art classes can become dreary after a while, so make sure you take the whole summer into account as you plan.

If your children are old enough for overnight camps, don't feel snubbed if they opt for these rather than going away with you. After all, you get to see plenty of each other the rest of the year. In fact, many fathers plan separate vacations with other adult companions. You need time away from your children, too.

Vacations should be considered in light of the children's activities as well as your work. Either make plans for the week a special children's program occurs, or else don't enroll the children in that particular program to begin with. A luxurious week may be much better for you all than a tightly budgeted 2-week vacation. Even without a wife, you are still eligible for family-plan travel breaks.

Clothing

The old days convey thoughts of children wearing the same clothes year after year. Hems were let down, seams taken out, the fabric seemingly resistant to any amount of wear and tear. It is not like that any more. Children are unlikely to wear even the big outer garments like coats for more than a couple of seasons. Buy jeans you can turn up the hems of, sweaters you can push up the sleeves of, under shorts loose on the waist. But bear in mind you can never get to the point where you can stop buying clothes for a prolonged period. Several pairs of cheap shorts and shirts are much more useful than a few fancier ones. Each child needs only one really presentable outfit to go out on the town. Don't waste your money buying fancy clothes which hang in the closet. Make a point of buying good-quality shoes (which does not mean expensive ones) for everyday wear and cheap ones for glamorous occasions. While you will not want to go along with foolish and endless requests for all the clothes in vogue, recognize how much it means to a child to be one with favored peers.

A father soon learns the importance of buying clothes children prefer to those he prefers. Don't go overboard buying summer clothes. Cut-off jeans and T-shirts are standard wear. Swimming suits occasionally can be worn throughout the day. Plan to discard old summer clothes in September as your child will have outgrown them come next June. Try to locate a well-to-do family with well-behaved children 2 or so years older than yours. They probably have quality clothing still in good shape that their children outgrew and may willingly sell or give them to you.

Just before the start of school is a good time to buy fall clothes and school supplies. Paper, pencils, and other needs—including clothes—go on sale at very reduced prices around the beginning of August. Stores generally tape a list of requirements for the different grades in a visible spot. Instead of buying the stipulated two pencils, buy a dozen; the best deal you can on spiral notebooks. No child has been known to mention that extra supplies are needed Monday until about 9 pm on a Sunday.

The original Scout motto, "Be Prepared," is something to have on your lips and in your ears. It is a great motto, but very hard to put into practice. The more successful you are, however, the greater are your chances of looking forward to coming home each day instead of dreading it.

11

Budgeting

Jane Manaster

At some point you have to sit down and figure out how the divorce and your new life style influence your financial situation. This will not necessarily allow you to end up rich or even solvent. However, unless you work within a budget and recognize how much money comes in and how it goes out, your money simply evaporates, and you will find yourself an anxious man. Ignore the rest of the world's boasts and bravados. When you hear people discussing college savings' accounts, new cars, or trips to Acapulco, tune them out. Chances are they have their woes too. Your monthly financial commitments, added to the incredible cost of day-to-day living, will keep you busy enough without your adding pipe dreams to your list of chores.

Understand right from the start that your pay check will not rise as fast as the cost-of-living index. One less mouth to feed—now that you are no longer married—does not materially decrease the amount of food or fuel consumed, or wear and tear on the home. Your children may find part-time jobs, but these are likely to provide pocket money for them rather than a new source of income for you. Additionally, large clothes cost more than small clothes, orthodontists more than routine dental checkups. Second-hand tricycles are cheaper than 10-speed bikes, and even first grade crayons and round-edged scissors are a giveaway compared with the school supplies needed a few years later.

Organizing your budget will not produce miracles, so don't hope you will ever be able to sit back smugly certain that both ends will meet. There will still be months when the car needs a new gas pump, an ear infection demands a 2-week supply of antibiotics, the tricky toilet suddenly floods the adjoining rooms. However, knowing ahead the amount of funds likely to be available, which bills can be juggled and paid a little later, and that a week's vacation can still be fun if it only lasts 4 days are defenses against insanity and the threat of bankruptcy.

With the pencil you hid behind the plates, and the utility bill envelope, start listing your current financial obligations (or you may choose to use the list provided at the end of this chapter). You may get 10% of the way into the list before you run out of space and realize what an undertaking this is. Then start again, and keep at it. Apart from the frequent expense of food and clothing, your routine monthly payments are likely to include a rent or home payment, utilities, gasoline and transportation, children's extracurricular classes, insurance, alimony and/or child support, and if you are buying larger items on time, these payments. Quite likely, you will also have to dig into your pocket for car repairs, doctor and dentist bills, prescription drugs, household repairs, entertainment, children's allowances, and birthday parties, and on a less menacing level, haircuts, kitchen supplies (cleaning agents, paper goods, etc.), bathroom supplies (toothpaste, toilet paper, soap, replacement combs, toothbrushes), pens and pencils, light bulbs, shoe repairs, dry cleaning, and birthday and holiday gifts and cards.

Next, take into account the things which make the difference between existing and living—candy and soft drinks, beer, cigarettes, magazines, the additional dollar or two for school field trips, purchases from door-to-door solicitors from Scouts or the school band. This last is important. Once you have a bad name in your neighborhood, you might as well move. While trying to save money, don't compromise yourself by getting too involved in baby-sitting pools, buying co-ops, starting a vegetable garden, that seem initially exciting ventures but which will absorb your free time. Running a job and a family leaves you precious few hours to relax. Spending those hours caring for other people's children or weeding the potato patch is not worth the effort. Or put another way, penny pinching is fine and dandy if it actually saves (such as buying day-old bread) but not if it costs (like baking your own bread weekly). Your earning power is worth more than the time spent kneading and sweating.

Your current needs are going to fall into several categories. First, the actual cost of your divorce and the ensuing alimony and/or child support. By now, the financial cost of the divorce will be apparent. Besides meeting your financial obligations to your former wife, you have lots of money involved in your children's welfare. If you share joint custody, it will not simply be a matter of whose turn it is to have the children under their roof. You also must consider how the expenses are split. Who will buy the bicycles, and winter coats , or pay for the summer camp, the medical and dental bills, and other major costs? Later, there may well be orthodontists, private music lessons, and long-distance school trips (the theater week in New York, the wilderness week in Colorado, for instance) and the trips to visit the distant parent or relatives.

Before stepping too far into the future   though, there is tomorrow and even today to be considered. One third of the day children are in school and one third they are asleep. This leaves about 8 hours of the 24 to be covered. If your children are not old enough for school, then you have much more time to account for. Shop around for day-care centers, nursery schools, and after-school care. Take a couple of sick days off from your job, use your phone to tap all resources, and learn what your community has to offer. Seek suggestions from other fathers and mothers who have children of similar ages.

Older children can come home and fend for themselves—provided you call each afternoon to check that they have arrived home, and get them in the habit of always letting you know where they plan to be. Community schools and city recreation centers usually have enough going for children that they enjoy these at least a couple of afternoons a week.

The cost of your home will be a major monthly expense, and if divorce necessitates a move, choose with great care. How much space do you really need? How many bathrooms? How big a yard? Is an apartment cheaper than a house? Would the switch from a large house to a small apartment unhinge the children's stability? Or would they enjoy it? A swimming pool on the premises and the availability of someone to jump rope or play soccer with means much more to a 9-year-old than the lawn that has to be mowed and the extra space to be kept clean and tidy.

Your home costs are not only the actual square footage, but also utility bills, the upkeep and taxes and the insurance. It is advisable to live in a socioeconomic neighborhood comparable to the one you had before to facilitate the change. If you have joint custody, find a home nearby and close to the children's schools, friends, and recreation centers. But beyond that, the field is open. Even if you have lived all your life in a four-bedroom, two-story house with a garden, and a double garage, you and your children may be much better off in an apartment complex with a swimming pool where your social life and social support system are pleasurable. Money saved on accomodation can be spent elsewhere, and children are infinitely more adaptable than we often give them credit for. The parent who stays home feeling virtuous about offering the fresh-baked after-school snacks often has been shocked to learn that their children wish to go to the church hall where all their friends go and receive Kool-Aid and crackers!

Utility bills need constant monitoring. Train yourselves to switch off lights, not to stand gazing in the refrigerator, to keep the home temperature bearable rather than ideal, and to leave the drapes drawn or open to help rather than impede the heating or air-conditioning. The frequent use of air-conditioning is giving away to the use of overhead fans. Put the stopper in the sink, and let little kids share the bathtub. Restrict teenagers (who never washed anyway until they hit puberty) to one shower a day instead of allowing a pre-school, pre-game, and pre-date one.

Instead of keeping a room for visiting grandparents and the children's friends, buy a convertible hide-a-bed sofa, sleeping bags, and a couple of extra pilllows. It's remarkably cheaper that way. Your own bedroom can serve perfectly well as your study or office, unless the tax break makes an extra room worthwhile (which is usually not the case anymore). Home insurance, like other kinds needs attention. Call several companies, and have their policies spelled out carefully. Don't be afraid of asking the same questions over and over; the insurance business is highly competitive and the best deal should receive your business rather than the best salesperson.

This applies to life and medical insurance too. Don't be bamboozled into buying a massive life insurance policy so that your children grow up longing for your demise instead of relying on your personal help in developing their skills and attitudes toward a successful life. Make sure you have enough put by for unexpected medical expenses, but don't pay for your insurance agent's new Alfa-Romeo because you were scared into believing your children were on the brink of falling prey to mankind's worst diseases. Regular medical checkups, decent diet, and a home free from fire and poisoning hazards raise your children's chances of reaching maturity much better than high insurance premiums. If you get landed with a bad insurance deal, change it. It is entirely possible that the several hundreds of insurance dollars you have been paying each year, or plan to pay, can be better invested through your bank.

Check out the savings options available to you. While it is unlikely that you have a lot of unused cash right now, remember the old-world wisdom that two dollars saved is better than two dollars overspent. If your budget will not allow grandiose savings, do the best you can anyhow.

Although savings are usually earmarked for rainy days or some vaguely specified needs in the future, they are likely to be dug into for vacations and the occasional splurges all of us need to maintain our sanity. Family holidays work out best when there is a good chance everyone will enjoy the trip.

Find the best deals in both travel and accomodation. If you are lucky enough to live within the reach of the train track, and plan to travel some distance, check out their family plan. Overnight in a reclining seat is perfectly fine, an adventure children seem to thrive on, and an amazingly good value. Take food along, of course, to maintain the savings, but be generous with allowing purchases of drinks and snacks. If your own travel ticket and your hotel room can be worked into a business trip, the whole idea becomes more feasible. Check into the various discount fares for children and pre-payment. Long distances on the bus can be grim, especially if your children are young and need to move around plenty. Don't be seduced by the price of tickets; count the cost of temper. Most of the hotel chains accomodate children free, charging extra for roll-away beds. Some will furnish you with a kitchenette, leaving you the choice of saving on restaurant meals.

All vacations cost money, of course, but some of the cheaper ideas include camping, hosteling, and staying with tolerable relatives. Young children are hateful when overtired so don't push them excessively. Also remember to figure out just how much money you can afford to spend and where it will stretch best.

Two alternatives to a family vacation are sending the children to overnight camps (ranging from the Scout variety to the considerably higher private kind) or, if no ex-spouse or other relative is available, paying someone to mind the youngsters while you take off by yourself for a few days. Don't feel guilty indulging yourself. The children will love you better rested and relaxed.

In fact, as you work through your budget, don't exclude yourself from personal spending. Allow yourself an hour in the middle of the day with friends. You are not paying for a baby-sitter at this time, and the price of a lunch, combined with the pleasure of adult company, will reduce your harried houseperson feeling.

Budget for your own recreation. Your subscription to a sports or social club allows you the dual identity of a grown-up man and a housekeeper. It is a false economy to relinquish your own recreational preferences to save a few bucks a year. For the children, you will find skating, bowling, and movies usually worth the money. The franchise birthday-club hamburgers, ice creams, and free breakfasts are a good excuse for family outings. Other economical social activities include gatherings at your church (try and join one, even if your faith has lost out lately), PTA, community school and single-parent groups. Potluck suppers are often featured, so master a couple of dishes and participate with pride.

Make sure you do not miss out on inexpensive activities because of transportation cost. If you choose your home carefully, your children can learn to get around on bicycles, on city buses, and (even though they may need some convincing) on foot. Very few children nowadays believe or care that Abraham Lincoln walked 7 miles to and from school each day. Your urging them to walk may need something more up to date as an incentive.

You will, of course, have to get to work each day, so be sure your budget includes transportation, and any special work-related clothes, as well as all the extras like birthday and Christmas presents for your fellow workers.

There are two major costs yet to be figured: clothes and food. Clothes are not as bad, so start with them.

Buy your children enough of everything they need to carry them through a week plus a couple of days (in case you can't face the laundromat): 10 pairs of underwear and socks, a drawerful of T-shirts, at least four pairs of pants (mostly jeans), a sweater or two, sturdy sneakers, a pair of inexpensive church shoes, clothes to look cool in, a good-quality winter coat, gloves and hat, swimsuits, shorts, and, for daughters, a few dresses. These are the basics.

It matters a whole lot to children that they wear the "in" clothes, so while your money may not run to the latest down vest, an appropriately emblazoned T-shirt is a terrific booster. April is a good month for sales in men's and boys' clothing, August for school clothes. The major sales after July 4th and Christmas are probably the best time of all to buy. Never buy impulsively. Be considerate with children's high-fashion items. When you were a kid, no one cared too much. Now they do. To a certain extent you can buy clothes to last 2 or 3 years, but American manufacturers are not inclined to favor this, and few garments are made with substantial hems or seams that can be let out. You can buy too-long jeans and staple the hems up to begin with, but don't spend a lot of time trying to work out ways to make clothes last forever. Better hand down your children's too smalls, and pick up larger children's clothing either through a neighborhood pool, cousins, or even garage sales. Don't be too proud to buy secondhand; be realistic.

The hardest part of your budget is going to be food, because it costs a lot of money and has to be purchased constantly. Reckon on about 20% of your monthly costs going on food, and if this sounds, high, then bear in mind a recent figure quoted on the amount of income budgeted for food in urban India—84%.

The usual recommendation is that you do not impulse buy, but be prepared to go wild every now and then, buying a can of artichoke hearts, decent salami, French wine, or whatever takes your fancy. The thought of life being itemized from here on is depressing. But apart from keeping enough in your piggy bank for the occasional splurge, you will have to organize your food purchases. How many meals will there be a week? Say seven breakfasts, two home lunches, three sack lunches, and two school ones for the children, 13 dinners in 2 weeks (so that the 14th night can be taken away from home).

If you can organize yourself enough, you are best off making one major trip to the supermarket each week. When you see experienced shoppers doing this, it looks like a cinch. Don't be fooled; it is not at all easy to by a lot in one trip. Rather than aim for 100% success, try and check out the breakfast-cereal situation, the cookies and snacks, the frozen-food compartment of the refrigerator—or your freezer—the shelf with canned goods, and your dry goods like spaghetti and rice. Keep a list in your kitchen of items you use. After each meal take a moment to jot down the foods you finished. When you throw away a bread wrapper, add that item to your list.

Meat, fish, and chicken may account for a third of your spending. Scour the Wednesday and Thursday papers for specials and take advantage of sales. Stock up also during sales of canned or frozen foods, and, of course, on meat which you will have to rewrap properly before freezing. Don't buy a whole lot of perishable items as they simply will be wasted. Cheap margarine tastes like reconstituted axle grease, cheap cookies like sawdust, and the left over meat that is marked down is often overly endowed with fat or gristle, so be very watchful. Try to find time to visit two major stores weekly as the different companies vie for business and offer reduced lines each week.

Bruised fruit is worth looking at as you can dig out the unsightly bits, but don't be dumb enough to buy 8 pounds of brown bananas for 50 cents because there isn't anything you can do with brown bananas except make loaf after loaf of banana bread which will take up the rest of the day.

Buy in quantity where practical. A gallon of corn oil, which can sit quietly under the kitchen sink, is cheaper than if purchased by the quart, and if you fry, or make your own salad dressing, it will be gone in a matter of months. Are potatoes cheaper in 20-pound bags than 5-pound ones? Almost the worst smell in the world is a rotten potato, so when you think something crawled into the kitchen and died, this is probably what it is.

As your time will be at a premium, you will not want to sit down studying wordy diatribes on budgeting. However, two very concise booklets available from the Superintendent of Documents, U.S. Government Printing Office, Washington, D.C. 20402, will be worth the price of the stamp, and the minimal charge now required.

Food for the Family—a Cost-Saving Plan, prepared for the Department of Agriculture by the Science and Education Administration, is No. 001-000-03884-2, and outlines very clearly how much food to buy and serve, how to plan low-cost meals, and offers sample shoppping lists. Simple recipes also are included.

Covering a broader spectrum, *Managing Your Money—a Family Plan*, can be read in a matter of minutes, though you will want to turn to it more closely, and likely heed the recommendations given on drawing up a budgeting plan.

If, however, you do enjoy spending an evening reading more extensively into this area, head your list with, *How To Cope with the High Cost of Living*, by Sidney Margolius and Conrad Brown; published by Creative Home Library, in Association with Better Homes and Gardens. As well as including tips for daily expenses, there are chapters on repairs and additions to your home.

Assuming the more usual circumstances that by the time you have fixed breakfast, worked all day, come home and fixed dinner, helped with homework, laughed along with the family at a couple of sitcoms, and tackled the children's bedtime, even the evening newspaper is beyond your powers of concentration, here are a few tips in household saving which have minimal failure rate:

Learn minor repair skills such as replacing bicycle tire tubes, fixing stopped-up toilets, sewing on buttons. Trade off your skills with your neighbors.

Car pool.

Hit garage sales for everything from clothes to pots and pans. Saturday-morning early birds get the pick of the sales.

Check out eligibility for tax breaks, school-lunch programs, additional financial allowances for being a single parent.

Share garden and repair tools as often as practical.

Buy Christmas cards and wrapping paper, Valentine cards, etc., when they go one half price the day after the event...if you usually buy a lot, or are chintzy.

See movies at twilight shows rather than at expensive hours.

Study the local paper for the best entertainment values and restaurant coupons.

Pick up magazines from the "freebie" table at your public library—introduce the idea if no one did already.

Milk until dry every local resource offering recreational facilities, leisure courses, and sports amenities.

Free dog bones make good soup stock.

Buy all bakery products at the day-old outlets: terrific saving!

Keep wasteful household goods (like paper towels) to a minimum.

Buy goods in quantity only when they will be used.

If you keep in touch with relatives by long-distance, make the calls on weekends or (if your children are too talkative) late at night.

Share money-saving discoveries. It's fashionable to boast poverty.

In general, a sharp shopper

- shops with a definite purpose in mind

- compares price and quality

- examines the merchandise carefully

- shops at the start of a sale

- selects irregulars and seconds with unnoticeable defects

- considers manufacturers' close-outs

The following sales calendar comes from a Texas Agricultural Extension Service pamphlet published by Texas A&M University (as do some of the above suggestions):

January: "white sales"—towels, sheets, pillowcases, blankets; furs; winter clothing; furniture; jewelry; Christmas cards and decorations; store-wide clearances.

February: home furnishings, rugs, mattresses, housewares, china, glassware, silverware

March: garden supplies, spring clothing, luggage

April: after-Easter sales; women's coats, suits and accessories; men's and boys' clothing

May: lingerie, handbags, television sets, soaps and cleaning aids, automobile tires

June: ladies' ready-to-wear, television sets, fabrics

July: summer clearances after July 4th, sporting goods, sportswear, hosiery, women's hose, floor coverings, summer furniture, shoes, appliances, used cars

August: clearance of summer clothing, back-to-school specials, children's play clothes, furniture clearances, yard and gardening equipment, "white sales"

September: back-to-school specials, housewares, fabrics

October: hosiery, lingerie, fabrics

November: pre-Christmas promotions, ladies's coats and dresses

December: general store clearance after Christmas with markdowns on toys and gifts; winter clothing late in the month

You must recognize that just when you get your household in order, and everything arranged to work smoothly, you may meet a fine woman and wish to marry again. Before taking the big step, sit down again with your pencil and calculate how your alimony, child support, home and living expenses will be changed.

Developing a Budget

Now, while you still hopefully are solvent, think about how much money you will take in and how you will spend it. By proper planning at this time you may reach a position where your income matches your spending. Give it a try.

	Jan.	Feb.	Mar.	Apr.	May	June	July	Aug.	Sept.	Oct.	Nov.	Dec.	Total amount planned to spend	Total amount actually spent
Food (home and away)														
Housing (rent, insurance, mortgage, repairs)														
Utilities (heating and cooling														
Child support (with mother, with you)														
Alimony														
Legal Fees (divorce-related, new will, etc.)														
Child care (daily, weekends)														
Clothing (purchases, repairs)														
Cleaning (house, clothes)														

	Jan.	Feb.	Mar.	Apr.	May	June	July	Aug.	Sept.	Oct.	Nov.	Dec.	Total amount planned to spend	Total amount actually spent
Health (insurance, doctor and dentist bills)														
Education (tuition, books supplies)														
Transportation (bus, auto, from home to home)														
Personal (allowances, haircuts, tobacco, drinks)														
Recreation (movies, vacations, hobbies)														
Contributions (church, door to door)														
Insurance (life, accident, property, sickness)														
Savings (bank, bonds, securities)														
Taxes (income, auto, personal property, sale of estate)														
Dues (local unions, professional associations)														
Debts (appliances, auto, clothing, credit cards)														

Index

Adjustment patterns in divorce
  Children's, 71–72, 74–80
  fathers', 32–38
Adolescents, 25, 62–63, 72, 79–80, 112
Adversary system, 128
Affiliation
  in children, 56
  in divorced fathers, 45
Alimony, 20, 22, 93, 124, 138, 139, 150, 155, 156
Annulment, 132
Anxiety (*see* Personality disorders)
Autonomy, 45, 56

Baby sitters (*see* Sitters)
Behavior
  stress-revealing, 86–92
  understanding children's, 52–53
Boys, special problems of, 69, 71, 76–77
Budgeting, 179, 186–196
  form for developing, 196
  sales calendar, 194–195

Camps, 183
Child support, 20, 22, 93, 148–149, 155–156

Children
  basic needs, 53–57, 77
  father's role in meeting, 57, 64
  growth and development, 58–63
  and holidays, 24, 125, 181–183
  predivorce, 67–68, 81–84
  preferences in custody, 147 (*see also* Custody)
  rights of, 106
  and stages of divorce, 68–70
  therapy for, 49
Cleaning services, 176–177
Clothing
  budgeting for, 190–191
  buying, 183–184
  care of, 177
Commitments, keeping, 98
Communicating, 99
Community property rule, 149
Congruence
  in children, 57
  in divorced fathers, 46
Contempt of court, 152
Contested divorce, 134–135
Control
  in children, 56
  in divorced fathers, 45
Co-parenting (*see* Custody, joint)
Counseling, 131–132
  (*see also* Therapy)

Consistency, 97–98
Custody
change of, 115, 125–127, 156–159
disputed, 153–154
and legal system, 126, 127–128, 156–159
patterns of, 14, 15, 22, 58, 105–122, 143–144
joint, 107, 118–122
sole, 106, 108–115
split, 106, 115–118
in trial separation, 132, 157

Day-care centers, 71, 178, 187
Denial, in children, 83–84, 86–87, 89
Depression (see Personality disorders)
Discipline, for fathers, 10
Divorce
alternatives to, 131–132
and career problems, 21
and contemporary family life, 14–16
effects on women, 69, 71
legal factors, 19–20
(see also Custody)
preparing for, 29, 81–84
stages of, 38–40
statistics, 27
time effects, 23–25
types of, 14, 107, 128, 133–135, 143
Domestic tasks, 20–21, 38–70
(see also Food, Clothing, House-cleaning, Meals)

Elementary school children, 25, 60–61, 71–72, 78–79, 113
differing impact of divorce on boys   and girls, 72
Emotional support
in divorce, 18, 20, 71–72
in marriage, 17

Families
healthy, 17, 19

supportive role, 91–92
Fathers' rights groups, 111, 137
Finances, 21, 113, 117, 123–124, 142
(see also Budgeting)
Food
basic list, 168–171
groups, 163
shopping for, 191–192
Food for the Family—a Cost-Saving Plan, 192–193
Foreground-background technique in problem solving, 12–13

Games, 182–183
Girls, special problems of, 73–74

Habeas corpus actions, 152, 154
Home size and location, 187–188
Housecleaning, 176–177
How to Cope with the High Cost of Living (Margolius & Brown), 193

Illness in children, 174–175
Infants
effects of divorce on, 77
growth and development in, 59
Insurance, 188–189

Judges, 138, 144
Jury trials, 139–140, 144

Kitchen supplies, 169, 171–173

Lawyers
and adversary system, 128
attitudes toward custody, 144
choosing, 136–137, 139
and contested divorce, 134–   135
fees, 138
and uncontested divorce, 133–134, 135–136

Managing Your Money—a Family Plan, 193

Meals, preparing, 164-167
Mediation, 132
Medicine cabinet supplies, 176
Mothers
    relationship to sons in divorce, 69,
    71, 76-77
    and sole custody of young
children,   106, 113, 114
    working, 107

"No-fault" divorce, 14, 107, 128,
133,   143
Nutrition, 162-163, 167

Parenting, effective
    before divorce, 93-96, 146
    following divorce, 96-102
Pendente lite hearings (*see*
Temporary   hearings)
Personality disorders, 87-88
Preschoolers, 25, 60, 71, 77-78
Problem solving
    for children, 55
    for divorced fathers, 12-13, 44
Professional help (*see* Therapy)
Property division, 149-150)
Psychological problems of divorced
    fathers, 30-32

Remarriage, 41-42
    and custody, 157
    effect on children, 73-74, 126-127
Role models, 110

Safety, rules for home, 173
Savings, 189School
    children's behavior in, 88, 90, 101
    extracurricular activities, 179-180
    parent visits, 179
    transportation, 178-179
Sitters, 178, 181
Socializing, after divorce, 23
Stepmothers, 73-74
Stimulation
    in children, 57
    in divorced fathers, 46

Stress, in children
    signs of, 86-91
    in community, 90
    at home, 89
    in school, 88, 90

Teachers, and signs of stress in
    children, 88
Teenagers (*See* Adolescents)
Temporary hearings, 142-143, 147
"Tender years" doctrine, 106, 107
"Terrible Two's," 59
Therapy
    for children, 49
    selecting a therapist, 48-50
    when to seek, 47-48

Time
    children's perceptions of, 25
    in the divorce process, 29
    and the divorced parent, 23-25
    spent with children, 80-81
Trial separation, 132

Uncontested divorce, 133-134
Uniform Reciprocal Support Act,
155

Vacations, 183, 189-190
Visiting rights
    change of, 111, 127, 154
    and child support, 155
    disputed, 31, 111, 153
    effect on children, 22
    routines, 112
    and sole custody, 155
    in trial separation, 132

Weekends, 180-181

DATE DUE

A